MW00355029

BASKETS
IN
POLYNESIA

BASKETS IN POLYNESIA

by Wendy Arbeit
with photographs by Douglas Peebles

A Kolowalu Book
University of Hawaii Press
Honolulu

to my parents,
Carl and Ethel Arbeit,
who made it all possible

© 1990 University of Hawaii Press
All rights reserved
Printed in the United States of America
90 91 92 93 94 95   5 4 3 2 1

Library of Congress Cataloging-in-Publication Data

Arbeit, Wendy.
    Baskets in Polynesia / by Wendy Arbeit :
  with photographs by Douglas Peebles.
        p.   cm. — (A Kolowalu book)
    Includes bibliographical references.
    ISBN 0–8248–1281–6 (alk. paper)
    1.   Basket making—Polynesia.   I.   Title.
TT879.B3A7   1990
746.41'2'0996—dc20   89–20656
                                            CIP

University of Hawaii Press books are printed on acid-free
paper and meet the guidelines for permanence and durability
of the Council on Library Resources

Cover: Traditional coconut leaf basket from Fiji used by
women for collecting fish and shellfish

··CONTENTS··

Color plates follow page 6

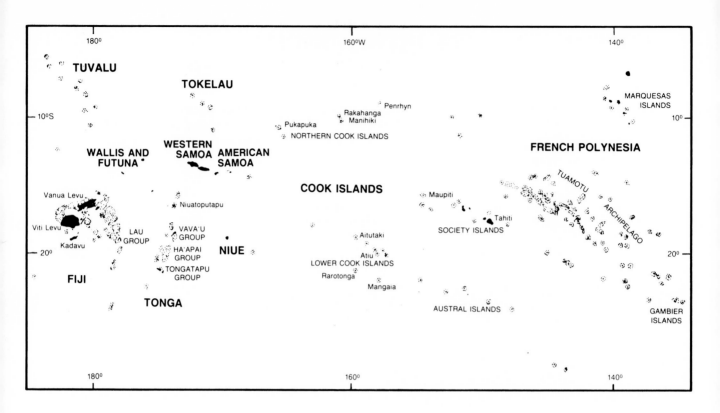
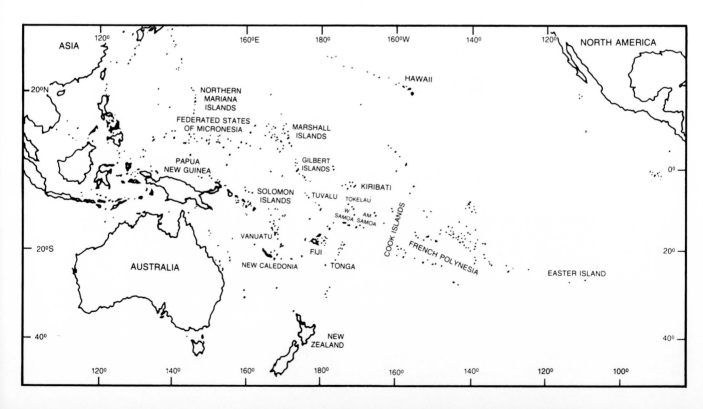

··FOREWORD··

Pacific basketry, in all its embodiments, is every bit as intriguing and worthy of appreciation as the more familiar art forms of the region, including wood and stone sculpture. Unlike basketry from North America and other parts of the world, however, Pacific examples of this near-universal material art are relatively unknown. No comprehensive study of Oceanic basketry has ever been produced, and there are few, if any, good contemporary accounts to parallel the vast and growing body of literature pertaining to Native American baskets and basket making. This present volume is an important first step in filling that need, and one that should focus much-deserved attention on this ancient Pacific tradition.

As the following pages show, the fiber arts are still very much alive in Polynesia and, for that matter, throughout the Pacific. Although the field collecting that forms the basis of this survey covers only a limited portion of what we today refer to as Polynesia (and Fiji), it is immediately apparent that basketry here is varied and complex, especially considering the overwhelming dependence on pandanus leaf and coconut frond as the major raw materials. It is also apparent, unfortunately, that many of the specialized basketry forms of the past are no longer remembered, casualties of changing lifestyles brought about by contact with the outside world during the last two centuries. While the fiber arts are still practiced with a keen sense of tradition as well as innovation, there is, nevertheless, cause for future concern. Many of the expert weavers of

Polynesia and other islands of the Pacific are women in advancing years, and without proper incentives for passing on their knowledge and skills, more and more is in danger of being lost. In celebrating the pride and persistence of this singular manifestation of human creativity in Oceania, this volume also pays tribute to weavers the world over.

When Captain Cook and his followers criss-crossed the Pacific in the eighteenth and early nineteenth centuries, they took scant note of the marvelous basketry creations found throughout the area. As a result, few baskets were collected and, being fragile, fewer still have survived to give us insight into the pre-European distribution of the various techniques and styles of manufacture and decoration. When professional anthropologists began making systematic collections in the early twentieth century, many forms had already been lost, others transformed, and new ones adopted. Thanks to collections that now repose in the Bishop Museum and other institutions worldwide, we at least have a baseline for understanding those changes that have occurred during much of this past century. By the same token, the collections and supporting information incorporated in this volume will add immeasureably to that understanding and provide a basis for comprehending the future of one of humankind's essential arts.

Roger G. Rose
Department of Anthropology, Bishop Museum

··ACKNOWLEDGMENTS··

Many people have contributed their time and knowledge to this project. Without their generous support the realization of this book would not have been possible. To all of you I extend my most heartfelt thanks.

In Fiji, the assistance of the Fiji Art Council and especially its executive secretary, Mereula Guivalu, was invaluable for including me in their farsighted program and sponsoring and arranging my visits to villages throughout the republic. Thanks also to the many Women's Interest Officers who graciously served as hostesses and interpreters and the sisters at St. Bede's School in Savusavu for their hospitality and assistance.

I had many knowledgeable advisors while in Tonga. Robin Coleman of Robin's Gift Shop steered me to all the villages in Vava'u known for their craftsmanship. Patricia Ledyard Matheson, remembered for her great good humor, has my thanks for introducing me to the women of 'Utulei and to Tu'ifua Fevaleaki, who generously shared her memories of Tongan plaiting in the recent past. In Nuku'alofa, Sa'ane Tupou of the Tongan Visitors' Bureau, Oto'ota Eva of the Langa Fonua, and Folau Taimikovi of Friendly Island Marketing Coop were generous in sharing their knowledge and resources. To Isabella Maka, I extend my thanks for her cheerful hospitality.

Apaula Brown, curator of the museum in Apia, Western Samoa, was kind in assisting me at a time when she was about to leave to attend a symposium. I am grateful to Dorice Reid of the Cook Island Tourist Authority and Maria Henderson for their concern, help, and information about Cook Islands baskets. The staff of the Tahiti Tourist Promotion Board in Pape'ete, Tahiti, I thank for identifying knowledgeable individuals and contributing recently displayed coconut frond baskets.

I am indebted to Jack H. Ward, John Meyer, and Niklaus Schweizer, all of the University of Hawaii at Manoa, for their guidance in linguistic matters.

For material on historical aspects of Polynesian basketry I depended largely on the facilities of the Bernice Pauahi Bishop Museum and the goodwill of its staff: Roger G. Rose, associate anthropologist/ethnologist, afforded me guidance in matters anthropological; Valerie de Beaumont, collections technician, cheerfully coordinated my access to the closed collection; Ruth Horie and staff at the museum library were most helpful in finding historical drawings. The workers in the Visual Collections Department, and especially Charlie Myers, did a wonderful job of making these ready for reproduction.

The manuscript was prepared on the computers at Honolulu Community College's Matsuda Center. Walter Chung was generous in allowing me access to the facilities there. Bill Langer at LabTech Hawaii, Inc., custom printed all black-and-white photographs, enhancing the already glowing images.

In matters of logic, elimination of obscure and ambiguous language, and just good sense, I am grateful for the sharp talents of my editors Iris Wiley and Betty Bushnell.

Most of all I owe a debt of gratitude to all the basket makers who unreservedly shared the secrets of their craft and spoke about their baskets and themselves. They proudly carry on an aspect of their cultural heritage that is fighting extinction. This book is about them and for them.

··PREFACE··

While gathering materials for my book *What Are Fronds For?* I was amazed and concerned to find that information on baskets of the Pacific basin is not readily available, but is scattered among such diverse sources as explorers' logs, missionary journals, ethnological monographs, and catalogues of museum collections. In addition, material is slim compared with that for such other industries as tapa making or boat building. Further, with the notable exception of Maori crafts, little about baskets has been added since the 1930s. It seemed to me that a craft so fundamental to the lives of Pacific Islanders deserved to be brought out of its literary obscurity. To begin to fill the need for an overview of two centuries of Pacific Island basketry, I set about preparing this book.

I decided to focus on the east and central portion of the South Pacific basin—sometimes referred to as central Polynesia. This region displays a uniformity of basket styles resulting from early migration patterns and subsequent recurrent voyages of a social, economic, or military nature. This uniformity exists along with subregional variations related most often to distances between the island groups. The islands of Fiji, located on the western extreme of tropical Polynesia, are included in this survey. Fiji has been classified as Melanesian by most researchers, but by others as Polynesian. In fact, it is in many ways a transition zone, its people and culture having characteristics of those both to the east and to the west of it. Perhaps due to its long and close association with Tonga and Samoa, in matters of basketry its place is more properly within the Polynesian sphere. Including it here provides a more comprehensive view of the similarity in certain basket forms and the successive change in others across the 7,000-odd-kilometer span of central Polynesia.

I have chosen to exclude the isolated "points" of the Polynesian triangle, New Zealand (Aotearoa), Easter Island (Rapa Nui), and the Hawaiian Islands, leaving to other researchers to investigate the plaiting traditions —especially as they relate to those of the central Polynesian homeland. The relationships certainly are intriguing. In Hawaii and Easter Island, coconut fronds, the most common basketry material elsewhere in tropical Polynesia, were not used for baskets. In New Zealand, where it is too cold for the palm to grow, the Maori devised equivalents of the coconut frond basket from their abundant flax. Pandanus, another widespread basket material in tropical Polynesia, was used for baskets in Hawaii but not Easter Island. Freycinetia and flax in New Zealand and bullrushes and banana stem skin in Easter Island were employed in those areas for plaiting flat satchels with bottom seams that are consistent with central Polynesian traditions. Twining was the basketry technique most commonly used in Hawaii, where it developed to a degree of sculptural complexity not found elsewhere in Polynesia. In New Zealand, the Maori used various kinds of twining to produce fabric rich in multicolored geometric patterns. Most remarkable was a kind of double twin-element technique. The same method was used by ancient Tongans in making their *mosikaka*.

In researching the antecedents of today's baskets, I studied literature available at the University of Hawaii's Hamilton Library and the library at the Bernice Pauahi Bishop Museum. Technical works on material culture, explorer and missionary journals, regional dictionaries, and unpublished manuscripts and field notes of Bishop Museum anthropologists provided much useful information. Complementing this were museum collections, especially those of the Bishop Museum. Other collections that proved helpful were housed at the Fiji Museum in Suva, Fiji, and Tupou College, just outside Nuku'alofa, Tonga. Still others have been tapped in a second-hand manner through photo reproductions of their artifacts in museum publications and file photos at the Bishop Museum.

To gain first-hand knowledge of the status of contemporary basketry, I spent six months in the major basket-producing areas of the region, collecting information and baskets. Most of my time was spent in Fiji and Tonga, where basketry activity is most vigorous.

Those baskets photographed on the following

pages are a representative sampling of both traditional and modern forms. Historical baskets were selected from the extensive collection of the Bishop Museum (color plate 7; figures 3, 17, 31, 34–39, 45, and 46; and photo on page 94), and contemporary ones, now part of that collection, were gathered by me in 1986 and 1987. All were expertly photographed in the studios of Douglas Peebles. I claim responsibility for all field photographs.

Tongan basket makers

··INTRODUCTION··

Before the people of the Pacific met those of Europe, every island woman spent a good part of her time plaiting. She plaited floor coverings, carrying and storage baskets, food wrappers, cooking containers, and special baskets for ceremonial events. In the eighteenth century intensive European exploration of the Pacific brought an end to the cultural integrity of the region. The introduction of European values, materials, and religions changed forever the Islanders' ways of living. As attitudes and economies changed, so did the nature of the artifacts made. No doubt the earliest changes were brought about by the choices explorers (the first Western tourists) made in collecting or trading and by the materials and objects they left behind. Thus began the chain of events in which plaited storage containers were replaced by trunks, ceremonial baskets were forgotten, and the free-for-the-picking natural leaf basket was rejected in favor of more prestigious, but costly, polyethylene bags, woven vinyl sacks, and Rubbermaid products.

The trend has its ironies. Artisans increasingly favor imported manufactured goods over their own handmade articles, while the foreigners who produce the manufactured goods seek out the very objects the craftsmen now reject for their own use.

Although gradual abandonment of local artifacts began about two hundred years ago, the most rapid changes have taken place in the last fifty years. Anthropologists writing in the 1920s and 1930s described coconut frond basket weaving as a functioning part of Polynesian culture. In the late 1980s, the only coconut frond baskets in general use were the simple ones, those made quickly and without prior preparation. Those requiring skill and time to make, when done at all, are mostly produced by women over the age of fifty. Pandanus baskets continue to be made, but not in the finer work of old.

There are a number of forces contributing to this trend: changes in cultural values, availability of money from relatives working locally or abroad, and difficulty of obtaining raw materials, to name a few. As persons from communal villages become absorbed into job markets, the need for farming and fishing baskets decreases. As children are educated for longer periods of time and frequently away from home, the conditions for passing on and continuing old traditions (including basketwork) are interrupted.

In general, younger women are now active basket weavers only where tourist traffic is heavy, and they weave new-style baskets, adapting older methods to the tastes of the modern purchaser. This home industry represents an intermediate step in the on-going shift from a communal to a monetary economy. In those places where the impetus to continue making baskets is strictly monetary, should artisans weaving for the tourist market find other kinds of employment more lucrative, even the evolving contemporary styles could disappear. All things considered, the outlook for the future of ethnic baskets would appear bleak indeed. However, a counter-trend is now beginning to develop: a reawakening of pride in local identity. Increased cultural awareness, growing appreciation of past accomplishments, and resistance to losing local heritage are emerging to coexist and perhaps compete with the movement toward adoption of foreign mores and economies. Still, whether the burgeoning cultural self-esteem will prove sufficient to foster a resurgence of traditional craft activity only time will tell.

Because the tropical island environment is hot and wet, baskets soon disintegrate once discarded. This means that no archaeological evidence of Pacific baskets is possible. Our knowledge of Polynesian baskets begins, then, with the collections made on the three voyages of Captain James Cook from 1768 through 1780. In the preface to her book "Artificial Curiosities," Adrienne Kaeppler explains: "Ethnographic collections from Cook's voyages are important because his voyages made the first extensive contact with Pacific peoples. It was not always the first contact, but it is the first contact from which we have collections that can be identified and studied."

The missions on which Cook was sent and which made these contributions possible were (1) to discover

Tahiti in the eighteenth century as pictured in
Hawkesworth's *Account*. Baskets are shown in use in
canoes, set on shore, and carried on a woman's back.
Photo courtesy of Bishop Museum.

the "great southern continent," (2) to enable the party of learned gentlemen who traveled with him to collect specimens and describe the regions they visited, and (3) to search for the fabled northern passage. While he failed to find those elusive geographic features, during his cruises Cook generated the most accurate and extensive maps and charts ever made of the Pacific Ocean. The innumerable natural history specimens and observations brought back by those on board transformed European knowledge of the Pacific. Sailing history, too, was transformed by Cook's dietary innovations which kept his crewmen free of scurvy, the vitamin C deficiency disease that in those days generally took the lives of as many as half the crew on a long-distance voyage.

Many thousands of ethnographic objects were collected by the early explorers, of which more than 2,000 are presently documented as having been acquired on Cook's voyages. Despite these sizeable collections of artifacts and the extensive descriptions of regions and peoples, we can gain relatively little information about the Polynesian baskets these early voyagers saw. Most of them regarded cultural artifacts as curiosities: curios. They brought back baskets that were given to them and that appealed to them, treating those artifacts as one might vacation souvenirs, without revealing the basis on which they were chosen or providing such information as source, use, materials, techniques, or exact origin. In fact Tahiti was often given as the place of origin for any Polynesian object. Early explorers and scientists rarely described the baskets they saw, surely in great variety. The plain baskets most typical of a culture were ignored altogether. This tantalizing comment by Georg Forster, a scientist on Cook's second voyage, is characteristic of early records. "The manufacturing of various baskets . . . in use among these natives is so multifarious, that a minute description of them would require too much time; so we must not therefore enter upon the detail. . . ."

We may wonder how those early observers could have failed to take advantage of the unique opportunity to learn about those newly "discovered" cultures before they were affected by alien influences. How could they have selected artifacts with the careless abandon of a tourist on holiday? Regarding baskets especially, there were many reasons. Basket weaving was women's work. It was still a common craft in Europe. Other Pacific basin crafts were more spectacular or fascinating. No one had responsibility for collecting material of a cultural nature. Gathering background information was difficult because of the repeatedly encountered language barriers. And finally, without the benefit of our excellent hindsight, they had no idea of the lasting impact their voyages would have on the populations they visited.

In the area of central Polynesia, Cook's ships visited Tonga, the southern Cook Islands, the Austral Islands, the Society Islands, and the Marquesas Islands. By far the greatest number of the baskets collected were from Tonga. We have no way of knowing if that was because other islands produced few baskets, because other artifacts from those other islands were more interesting, or because other artifacts from Tonga were less interesting. Neither can we assume that if a particular kind of basket was not collected it did not then exist. Objects collected on Cook's expeditions are now scattered among public and private collections throughout the world, with the majority among the holdings of the museums of Europe.

The next major collection of Polynesian baskets took place during the four-year expedition of the six ships of the United States Exploring Expedition (1838–1842). Its commander, Captain Charles Wilkes, had the mandate to sail the South Seas and chart and investigate the area scientifically. By the end of the voyage, the sailors and scientists had brought back more than 1,000 objects from Fiji and nearly 700 from the islands to the east of it. This collection represents a significant contribution to our store of knowledge. Once again no one person was charged with studying the island cultures and artifacts, and as a result ethnological information is largely random and anecdotal. The major part of this expedition's collection is now housed at the National Museum of Natural History, Smithsonian Institution, in Washington, D.C.

It was to be another eighty years before our knowledge of Polynesian baskets would be enlarged to any great extent. Between the years 1920 and 1935 scientists from Honolulu's Bishop Museum traveled to Polynesia to learn about it first hand. The ethnologists among them were the first to study the everyday baskets of the islands, recording their uses and methods of construction. Paramount among the researchers was Sir Peter Buck (Te Rangi Hiroa), born in 1880 in New

Zealand. His achievements include over one hundred monographs and articles about Polynesian cultures. Ethnologist at the Bishop Museum from 1927 to 1936 and director from 1936 until his death in 1951, he proved a significant force in the advancement of our knowledge of Polynesia.

A word about terminology. While basic technical or regional words relating to basketry will be explained at the time of their introduction in the text, there are three that require prior clarification. They are *plaiting, weaving,* and *braiding.* Plaiting is the best term available to describe the kind of basketry practiced in Polynesia. It indicates without further qualification the interlacing of sets of elements. In coconut leaflet plaiting, strips that are manipulated as warps in one row or section may be worked as wefts in the next. Strips may even turn 90° or 180° within the mesh to form corners. In pandanus plaiting, two sets of elements (the narrowed pandanus strips) are worked at right angles to each other and usually are placed at a diagonal to the artisan. One set of strips operates in concert. Like the warp, some of its elements are raised and others lowered to create a space called the shed into which a weft is set, then locked in place as the warp elements reverse their raised and lowered positions. The weft elements, which constitute the other set, are successively placed in each new shed. As plaiting continues, old warp elements are eliminated and new ones added.

Weaving is a specific form of plaiting. It utilizes two sets of elements (warp and weft) that are worked at right angles to each other. The warp always extends from one end of the fabric to the other and the weft interlaces across it. Any time there is dropping, adding, bending, or exchanging of warps, the technique is beyond the range of weaving and is properly termed plaiting. It is unfortunate that in common English the term weaving is often used in place of plaiting, as confusion can only result. I have attempted to use the word plaiting wherever appropriate, but where inconsistency with normal usage becomes disruptive, I have used the word weave or weaving.

Braiding is another specific form of plaiting. In braiding there are two multi-element groups that lie at a diagonal to the fabric edge. As each element reaches an edge, it turns and becomes a member of the other group. In French braiding, a technique used to bind or connect the elements that extend beyond the edges of the plaiting, an external element (emerging from the plaiting) is added to each just-turned braid element. A braid is free standing; a French braid is integrated into the fabric from which its elements originate.

Since there are those who have disparaged modern pandanus baskets—calling the worst of them airport art and the most insipid pan-Pacific—I feel that a look at the validity of this genre is in order. Modern-day baskets are the product of a circumstance where the makers are no longer the users and the users are from outside cultures. This results sometimes in lowered quality and often in eclectic designs, characteristics that are a normal and legitimate part of the on-going evolution of any living craft. Even those older forms that we may look on as classic, and consequently superior, did not emerge fully developed. They evolved, being altered in response to changing needs, new contacts, and migrations—but at every stage producing useful objects made with materials at hand. This continues to be true. The new-style baskets are useful to those who purchase them, and the money gained from their sale is useful to the makers. Artisans continue to use familiar techniques and materials while the needs and attitudes of the consumer affect aesthetics and quality. The most significant difference today is that the consumers are from a very different culture. Their knowledge, attitude, discrimination, and sheer numbers can have considerable influence on the nature of the development of local basketry styles. Yet, despite some uniformity in the nature of influences exerted by outsiders throughout the Pacific basin, distinct regional differences persist in the kind, quality, and even quantity of work produced. The craft of basketry is still very much under the control of the makers, and contemporary forms must be seen as a reflection of the enduring characteristics of each culture.

Distribution Of Polynesian Coconut Frond Baskets

Islands	Split Rib, Keel	1-Strip, Keel	2-Strip, Keel	4-Strip, Keel	'Ō'ini (number of kinds)	2- or 4-Strip, Round	1-Strip, 3-Braid	Multi-Segment	U-Shape
Kapingamarangi	=					x			x
Marshall	x		x						x
Gilbert	x	x	x		1				
Tuvalu	x	x	x				(x)		
Wallis and Futuna	x =		x						
Vanuatu			x						x
Santa Cruz	x o	x o	x					o	
Fiji	x =	x	x	x		x	(x)		
Tonga	=	x	x	x					
Samoa		x o	x	x	(1)	x	x	x	
Tokelau		x		x			(x)	x	
Northern Cook	−	x	x		(2)	x			x
Southern Cook	x o	x	x	x	(1)	x			
Tubuai	x		x	x	2				
Society	x −	o	x	o	8			x	o
Tuamotu				x	5				
Marquesas				x	1				
Mangareva				(x)					

Sources: Available collections and literature.

x   indicates closure by some kind of French braid combination.
( ) indicates a style believed by craftsmen to be one introduced in the twentieth century.
=   indicates a split-rib basket with non-continuous side plaiting.
−   indicates an unsplit-rib basket.
o   indicates a French roll closure.

Note: Santa Cruz baskets vary in detail from those found in Polynesia.

Plate 1. **Basketry materials in use.** *Top left,* Pandanus baskets in the market, Tahiti. *Top right,* Plastic coil market basket, Tonga. *Bottom left,* Vine sewing baskets, Fiji. *Bottom right,* Coconut frond 'ato, Samoa.

Plate 2. **Making temporary coconut frond baskets.**
Opposite page. Top left, Isu, Fiji. *Top right,* Kete,
Rarotonga. *Bottom left,* 'Ō'ini, Tahiti.
Bottom right, Kato, Tonga.

Plate 3. **Coconut frond forms.** *Top right,* Split rib basket,
Ha'apai, Tonga. *Center right,* Toy, Fiji. *Left,* Carrying
basket, Fiji. *Bottom right,* Fine mat, Tongatapu, Tonga.

Plate 4. **Saki (fish scoop). Lau, Fiji.**
Made of coconut leaf midribs, this scoop is twined and
wrapped with hibiscus fiber and sennit.

Plate 5. **No'e. Vanua Levu, Fiji.**
This traditional coconut leaf basket, used by women
for collecting fish and shellfish, is made of two strips of
narrowed coconut leaflets and bound with hibiscus
fiber string.
55 and 31 cm wide × 23 cm mid-bottom to top

Plate 6. **Purse. Southern Cook Islands.**
A contemporary pandanus purse with dyed hibiscus fiber
plaited on top of the horizontals. The strips in the outer
surface measure 4 mm and the double-layered check
lining 27 mm wide.
25 cm long × 12 cm wide × 19 cm high

Plate 7. **Kete ngahengahe. Rakahanga, Cook Islands.**
This coconut leaf satchel was made in 1930 by one of the
few women who remembered how to make it. It is
decorated with strips of dyed pandanus, pompons of
stripped hibiscus inner bark, and buttons of shell. This
style is no longer made.
23.5 cm long × 30.5 cm wide × 19 cm high

Plate 8. **Single-strip, 2-braid coconut frond basket.**
A traditional keel-bottom basket in the Samoan style
made in just a few minutes from one long strip from a
fresh coconut frond. Nearly identical baskets are made
throughout most of Polynesia.
55 cm long × 31 wide × 23 cm high

Traditional coconut frond basket. Tokelau.
Made for carrying rocks, this 2-strip basket is strengthened by the insertion of extra leaflets. The bottom is closed with two French braids.
45 cm long × 41 cm wide × 28 cm high

··CONSTRUCTION··

The two plants most widely and intensively used by Pacific island basket makers are the coconut palm and the pandanus. Wherever man settled in the tropical Pacific, these plants were cultivated. This continuity of use is even reflected in their names. Coconut is known as *niu* from Madagascar to the Marquesas, and cognates of the general term for pandanus are found from Fiji through French Polynesia: *vadra* in Fiji, *fā* in Tonga, *fala* in Samoa, *ara* in the Cook Islands, and *fara* in the Society and Tuamotu Islands.

Coconut

Much has been written concerning the coconut palm's contributions to those living in the lowland Pacific. Its uses are myriad: medicines, charcoal, drums, strainers, and oil are some of the products that have been made from its various parts. The leaves, measuring up to 6 meters long, have been fashioned into many useful objects, such as thatch, mats, fans, plates, cooking containers, and baskets. Versions of these objects have been made everywhere the coconut palm is found.

The coconut frond is unique among basketry materials in that the plaiting elements start out connected. More than 100 leaflets grow on each side of the firm woody rachis or great rib. Each of these 4–6-cm-wide leaflets has a strong but supple midrib connecting the two halves. The leaflets are easily split into narrower strips when desired and removed from the great rib either singly or in a continuous strip with just the desired thickness of remaining great rib connecting them. These characteristics have been fully exploited by Pacific Islanders, who have devised a great variety of baskets differing in complexity, durability, and style.

The simplest kinds are made for temporary use in only a few minutes at the time they are needed and at the place where the palm grows. They are plaited in a check pattern (that is, alternately passing under and over the crossing leaflets) with the leaflets in their widest mode, uncut and opened flat. The material and the basket style are ideally suited to each other; only fresh, still turgid leaflets are firm enough to be plaited opened

flat. These baskets are used immediately—usually for transporting uncooked food—and then discarded or used for trash. Once dry, they become brittle, with a coarse, open mesh. Open-leaf baskets are the only kind that men make.

Temporary baskets come in variations of only a few basic forms. The most common is found throughout the reaches of the southeastern Pacific and far beyond. It is made from a single strip of leaflets that has been pulled off the great rib, plaited into a cylinder, and pressed into an oval. The resulting slit is French braided closed in sometimes one, but usually two, passes to form a keel-shaped bottom (color plate 8). Most variations of this basket have to do with details in handling the ends of the braids.

Another common type of basket is made from a small segment of the frond. (A segment consists of an unsplit length of great rib and the leaflets that adhere to both sides of it.) First the leaflets are plaited; for some styles each side separately, for others in a continuous cylindrical surface. Next, the unplaited ends are combined, usually by two French braids. Last, the great rib is split to form the opening. This type, which I refer to

— frond

— base end
— great rib

— tip end

fruit

Figure 1. **Split-rib baskets.**
Both are used for carrying light objects on the day the basket is made, then discarded.
Left: **Ketekete. Bua, Vanua Levu, Fiji.** Closed with a 2-course French braid. *42 and 32 cm wide × 28 cm high*
Right: **Kete no te kai. Rarotonga, Cook Islands.** Closed with a 2-course French roll. *52 and 46 cm wide × 27 cm high*

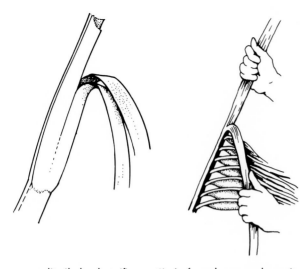

as a split-rib basket (figure 1), is found everywhere in Polynesia except Samoa, Tokelau, and the northern Cook Islands. The shape of the original plaited parts and the degree to which they are plaited together before braiding determine the final shape—flat and triangular, flat and rectangular, or somewhere in between. The basket may be plaited empty or around the contents to be transported. In the latter case the rib is not split until the final destination is reached. A major variation of this type, found only on Tahiti and the northern Cook island of Penrhyn, requires the great rib to remain unsplit in order to become the strong and rigid bottom. The opening is formed by a French braid that runs around the top edge of the cylindrical plaiting.

A third style, which I call by its Tahitian name, 'ō'ini, is confined to eastern Polynesia. The 'ō'ini is made from up to eight very short great rib strips whose leaflets are interconnected, then plaited. The way the strips are combined and the plaiting is conducted in regard to corners and top edge determines the number of openings (one or two) and the final shape—for example, spherical (figure 54), open and boxy (figure 53), or ovoid with a small opening. (See Willowdean Handy's *Handicrafts of the Society Islands* for detailed technical descriptions.) These small baskets are used for holding food in the underground oven and for carrying light loads.

An even less common temporary basket was found earlier this century on only a few of the Society Islands and in the northern Cook Islands. Today it is still made on the Marquesas island of Fatu Hiva. To make

this one, the middle two-thirds of the frond is scored in two places and bent into a U shape. The leaflet tips that are made to cross by this bending are combined into a French braid or roll on each side and then knotted together to form a handle (figure 4). Baskets with a slightly more developed form are in the collection of the Bishop Museum. Those collected from Kapinga-marangi in 1947 are similar to ones collected from Vanuatu in 1959, Pohnpei in 1946, and the Marshall Islands in 1945 and 1964, in that they have a triangular section of plaiting and two braids leading into the handles on each side.

Another temporary basket, found only on a few islands, is made from short segments of the coconut frond. These are plaited together to form a cylinder with the butt ends of the segments protruding from one edge and the leaflet tips from the other. Then the free leaflet tips are gathered together into a 2-course keel closing. This multi-segment basket has been documented for Samoa, where it is used to protect developing breadfruit, for Tahiti to carry cooked food, and (according to Buck) for Tokelau.

When a more durable, somewhat permanent basket is desired, the frond is carefully selected and cut several days in advance from among those fronds toward the top of the crown, those having little wind and insect damage and still in their tender youth. Even the choice of tree is important, as the leaflets must have the desired width and spacing along the great rib. The frond may be used as is, or wilted, or boiled, or drawn over an open fire to make it tougher and more supple. At a convenient time, the basket will be plaited in the village, then set out in the full sun to cure. Only women make permanent baskets. In fact, whenever I asked if men can make them, I was answered with peals of laughter. Permanent baskets are constructed from two or four long, narrow, flexible strips of leaflet-bearing great ribs with the leaflets closed (folded). Use of the folded-over leaflets produces a basket having walls twice the thickness of a temporary basket. The resulting lower ratio of width of leaflet material to midrib assures that the plaiting will dry with less shrinkage and that there will be a higher percentage of tough midribs in the resulting basket. Four-strip baskets are even more durable than their 2-strip counterparts since lengthwise splitting of the closed leaflets to one-half or one-third their original width causes the ratio of leaflet material to midrib material to become lower still. This kind of basket can last for years of repeated use. Permanent baskets are generally made in one or two twill patterns; check, when used, is confined to small bands at bottom and top. (A twill pattern is created when strips repeatedly pass over two or more crossing elements.) Construction of all the permanent baskets begins with combining the strips that have been removed from both sides of the great rib, then plaiting their leaflets into a continuous cylindrical surface.

The most common bottom contour is narrow and sharp, like the keel of a boat (figure 7). This shape is formed by the way the cylinder is closed. The cylinder is pressed into an oval and leaflets on opposite walls inclining in one direction are combined. Next, the leaflets inclining in the other direction are combined. When the leaflets are combined using French braids only (the most common technique), the outside surface is smooth (figure 8, right) and the braid is seen clearly on the inside (figure 56). When a smooth inside surface is desired, the leaflets from opposite sides cross each other before braiding. A single crossing produces a sharp bottom, and plaiting across more strips produces a flatter one. To form an outside braid that stands out in sharp relief, its leaflets must be crossed before French braiding is done. In eastern Polynesia the first group of leaflets is crossed, then both groups of leaflets are worked together as one in the final step(s), while in western Polynesia the outside braid is made from the second set of leaflets only. Although two is most common, up to five courses may be required to complete the keel closing. By controlling the width, twists, and number of strips in the finishing braids, a great variety of closings, both strong and decorative, may be created.

Another multiple-strip basket has a short, nearly cylindrical shape with a flat bottom. The bottom is finished by two French braids (figure 42) that close it in a kind of seam, or two or four free-standing braids (figures 12, 36) that close it at the very center. A third type is always made small and comes in two shapes: flat semicircular with a straight bottom (figure 10) and pouchlike (figure 11). In the central Polynesian area keel-bottomed baskets have been found everywhere; cylindrical flat-bottomed ones in Fiji, Samoa, and the Cook Islands; and pouch and flat semicircular ones in Fiji only.

A less common plaiting technique employed in creating multi-strip keel-bottomed baskets involves splitting the midribs from the leaflets and plaiting the elements separately. Examples have been found in Fiji (figure 7), Tongatapu, and Niuatoputapu (figure 18).

Instructions for many of the above baskets may be found in my book, *What Are Fronds For?* See the chapter entitled Techniques in this book for details on plaiting methods as they relate to various kinds of twills. Technical descriptions of baskets and their construction are included in many of the ethnographies listed in the bibliography.

The cordage often found attached to baskets can be made of pandanus strips, separated layers of wild hibiscus inner bark, or separated fibers of the coconut husk. The selected material may be twisted into two plies or braided in three, and may be used in its natural state or dyed black.

Pandanus

Pandanus can be found growing untended throughout the tropical Pacific. However, plants used for mats and baskets are generally cultivated in groves near an artisan's home, or in the bush by a village's garden or plantation. They are carefully tended, pruned, and replanted to keep the leaves long, unbent, and healthy. Weavers can identify many different kinds of pandanus by name according to color, size, and leaf shape. Each type, when dry, has distinctive color, texture, and handling characteristics. As with fine coconut leaf articles, pandanus is worked only by women.

Preparation methods depend on the kind of pandanus used and the local environment. Leaves are usually collected green, the thorns on the leaf edges and midribs stripped off, and the leaves dried in the sun. Where tidal flats are available, some kinds of leaves are also soaked for days in the sea. In other places they may be boiled for a short time in fresh water to make the leaves lighter in color and softer. When leaves are to be dyed black they may be buried in the mud of mangrove swamps or taro plots, then boiled with a mixture of leaves, barks, coconut husk fiber, or (in Tonga) roof tin. Tuvalu expatriates living near Suva told me they also soak the leaves with "sea lime" to shift the color to yellow, and then may take an additional step of boiling them with *noni (Morinda citrifolia)* root bark when red is desired.

Once the leaves have been prepared, they are

Pandanus leaf preparation. *Top,* Pandanus under cultivation. *Center left,* Cut pandanus ready for transport to village. *Center right,* Removing thorns. *Bottom,* Leaves set out to dry.

Figure 2. **Pandanus rolls.**
Rolls of pandanus leaves in shades of natural tan and dyed black. Fiji, Tonga, French Polynesia.

Placing pandanus leaves into a roll

placed in tight flat rolls (figure 2) and put away for later use. Just before use, the leaves are made more supple by repeatedly drawing them along the back of a knife or the edge of a large clamshell. They are then slit into strips of the desired width by use of a folded tin can lid, small knife point, or broken mussel or clam shell. In Fiji the very narrow waste strips left over from this process are used in making braided or plied rope.

The most common technique of working pandanus is plaiting. Techniques of plaiting baskets and satchels in checks, twills, repeat patterns, and figured motifs were well developed by the time of the earliest Western contact. As in earlier times, today the light tan leaf may be used alone or combined, as in Tonga and Fiji, with the natural brown *paogo (Pandanus whitmeeanus)* or with black-dyed leaf. In Tahiti the dark strips of wild banana bark are used for contrast instead. Pattern is emphasized in the southern Cook Islands by incorporating strips of the inner bark of the wild hibiscus *(Hibiscus tiliaceus)* colored with bright commercial dyes. The wild hibiscus is called *vau* in Fiji; *fau* in Tonga, Samoa, and the Tuamotu Islands; *au* in the Cook Islands; and *hau* in Tahiti.

Another way of making baskets with pandanus is to wrap and knot strips of it around coiling coconut leaflet midribs. The knotted wraps may be worked solidly in one color only (figure, page 111), in two or three colors to create geometric patterns (figure 22), or mixed with extra wraps to produce openwork designs (figure 3).

The history of the pandanus-wrapped coil basket in Polynesia is a mysterious one. These baskets were collected from Nauru, Samoa (figure 39), and the Tuamotu Islands before 1890, but without collateral information. Less than forty years later only conflicting information could be found. The Beagleholes wrote that the basket had been introduced into Pukapuka (northern Cook Islands) in the 1930s "from Samoa by the wife of the resident agent." Samoans told Buck that their openwork baskets originally came from Niue. Within the same decade Edwin Loeb was informed by natives of Niue that the technique had been introduced from Samoa. Those Niue baskets, however, were done in a double-face knot much like that used in Tonga today. The Samoan knots cross only in the front and the Tongan ones on both faces—hence the term "double face." In Tonga the technique is said both to have been

introduced from Niue and to have been devised locally. A card in the files of the Bishop Museum records Dr. Kenneth P. Emory's comments about a coil basket collected from Fakarava. It reads, "This is a Samoan form of basket which was introduced into the Tuamotus. A woman, over age 80, at Vahitahi, a native of Hikueru, told me in 1930 that she remembers when the basket came in. It was thought to have been introduced by some Manihiki natives." Similar solidly knotted baskets in German collections were acquired from the Tuamotu Archipelago before 1885. Today coil market baskets made and sold around Suva, Fiji, are believed to have been introduced by Tongans living there. Actually they are a combination of the solidly knotted Tongan style and the single-face Samoan stitch. Most not brought from Tonga are made by expatriate Tuvalu women.

Other Materials

Freycinetia arborea grows in the upland forest. It climbs to the tops of the tallest trees, trailing its aerial roots down to the floor below. These aerial roots with the bark removed are split into two or more parts and woven into very sturdy baskets. In Fiji this material is plaited into modern market baskets on the island of Vanua Levu and combined in a traditional 3-strand lattice-work technique into old- (figure 13) and new-style baskets on Viti Levu. Samoans fashioned it into twined fish traps, and in French Polynesia it was made into nearly spherical twined baskets. It is called *'ie'ie* in both these areas and *wamere* (among other names) in Fiji.

The tough stems of the high-climbing *Epipremnum pinnatum* are used to make the ceremonial baskets (figure 31) that have been observed in Tonga since the time of the earliest voyages. The vines are pulled down, rolled into coils, and brought to the village. There the bark is removed and the insides split and taken to soften in the sea. Eventually the basket is made using a technique that involves wrapping the strips around a spiraling core of coconut midribs. The plant, called *alu* in Tonga, still grows on the island of 'Eua and, to a lesser extent, Vava'u. This tough woody material is also found in the Caroline Islands where it is called *palu*, on Uvea where it is known as *halu*, and in Fiji where it has many names, *yalu* and its cognates being the most common. It is interesting that another Fijian name is *toga* (pronounced tonga). Alu baskets with the same

Figure 3. **1924 pandanus coil basket. Niue.**
The pattern has open areas as in Samoan work, but the
knot used is similar to the Tongan, which has its cross-
over on both faces.
14 and 26.5 cm wide × 16.5 cm high

shape and knotting technique were made in the past on all the above-named islands; but only in Tonga are they still made today, and in a continuation of one of the old styes.

Still other materials have been used to a lesser degree for making baskets. In Tonga a waterproof carrier was once made by stitching two fan palm leaves together. In Fiji many kinds of vines and aerial roots are used for twined fish traps and 3-strand lattice-work baskets. Tahitians continue the practice of using split bamboo to make a fresh fish holder. Cook Islanders use the outer skin of the stem of a tarolike plant for enhancing design in pandanus baskets. And the list does not stop there. Such materials as guava wood, fern stem, mangrove aerial root, and coconut leaf sheath fiber have all been involved in the construction of baskets.

Intimate knowledge of their environment traveled with islanders as they moved from island to island across the Pacific. In populations that became isolated, novel applications and techniques evolved differing widely from those of the mainstream, while in periods or regions of great nautical activity, the opportunity for sharing served to lessen some of those differences. The following chapters will indicate some of the ways in which baskets fit into this pattern.

Figure 4. **Fresh coconut leaf basket. French Polynesia.** U-shaped baskets of this kind have been made in French Polynesia with both French roll and braid seams. Slightly more evolved forms have been found elsewhere in the Pacific.
27 and 36 cm wide × 40 cm high

Figure 5. **Kawa. Kadavu, Fiji.**
Fish trap from village of Daveqele of *tokutolu* and *tuva*. It
is made and used by women. Traps made and used by
men are three times as large. Traps of the same shape are
found in Rotuma and Samoa.
30 cm wide × 21 cm high

Making a kawa

··FIJI··

In the fall of 1987 I visited rural villages on Fiji's three largest islands. My sponsor, The Fiji Art Council, selected villages renowned for their baskets and made advance arrangements for my visit. Since many of these areas had infrequent mail service and no telephones, despite our carefully laid plans, often notice of my visit would not have preceded me. I would arrive in the village with the Women's Interest Officer (the Fiji government field coordinator for women's affairs) and take everyone by surprise. One thing about Fijian ladies, they are gracious. Once they learned why I was there, coconut fronds would just appear—fresh-cut ones as well as sunned ones that had been prepared by weavers for their own use. Before I knew it, ten to twenty women would have gathered in their newest and brightest *sulu* (meter-long pieces of fabric printed in tropical patterns that are worn as skirts by simply wrapping around the body). After a kava ceremony with the chief of the village, we would assemble, usually outside in some shady area, seated cross-legged on pandanus mats.

As I photographed and asked questions, everyday life would go on. Children would run and tumble about us, and men passing on their way to their bush plantations would stop to have a look at what we were doing. Basket making would proceed with, to me, a surprising division of labor. We in the West are so precious about the things we make. Fijians enjoy the easy nonchalance of sharing. One person might thin the coconut leaflets, another twist the strips together, another plait the sides of the same basket, and still another braid the bottom; all this while teaching each other, nursing babies, and running to fetch still another sample basket to show me.

Late in the morning, quite a number of women would drift off one by one. Then, when lunch was announced, I would discover why they had left. We would all be ushered into one of the larger houses, usually belonging to the chief. There, down the middle of the completely pandanus-matted floor would be a long tablecloth almost covered with plates and plates of food. The ladies had gone to prepare our pot-luck party! It was hard to believe they hadn't expected me; the food was always incredible: taro, cassava, vegetables in coconut milk, crabs or fish caught just that morning, even Indian dishes of roti and curry.

After lunch our plaiting party would continue. Again glimpses of life: one lady would drop by to have company while she grated some coconuts; a teenager, having cut her hand, would run in with some medicinal leaves for one of the elders to apply; even a group of men might congregate with their big wooden kava bowl and coconut cups for an afternoon grog. Late in the afternoon we would quit, the day's pleasant activity having produced at least one fine basket per artisan, baskets that would last for months or years of hard use.

The nation of Fiji consists of two main high islands, Viti Levu and Vanua Levu, and ten island groups made up of more than two hundred small, mostly low, islands. Regional differences in the way coconut fronds are woven may once have existed between the interior and coastal areas of Viti Levu and between the various island groups; that would have been true in earlier times when chiefs held sway over narrow geographic areas and when there was considerable fierce warfare between them. But pacification and unification under the English in 1874 made it possible for Fijians to travel farther from their native villages in safety and then to marry others from increasingly distant regions. It is the custom in Fiji for a woman to move to her husband's village. Normally she will then adopt the plaiting styles of that place. But if she makes baskets and the women in her new home plait little or not at all, which is increasingly now the case, she will continue weaving, and in the manner she has learned. So, it is possible today to find a woman making baskets not in the style of her husband's village where she resides, or even in the style of the village of her birth, but in that of her mother's birth village. A fortuitous side effect is that the transplanted bride may be a source of revitalization of basket making in her new home.

Of all the islands in the eastern Pacific, Fiji maintains the strongest link with its weaving past. Wherever you go in Fiji, from the most remote rural area or iso-

Top left, Woman and child with noke. *Top right,* Boy with isu. *Bottom left,* House interior. *Bottom right,* Woman using kato.

lated atoll to the nation's capital, you see locally made baskets in use; by men, by women; by Fijians, by Westerners—by anyone who needs to gather, carry, store, fish, shop, or give a gift. The great majority of these baskets are made from the coconut frond.

Common work baskets are made in quite a variety of styles. Most common is the rough *isu* (top right photo on page 19), a split-rib basket with a difference. After the leaflets on both sides of the great rib are woven to triangles, those two are brought together and the leaflets connected into a French braid on each side. What distinguishes the isu from the split-rib basket found elsewhere is the final shaping. Before tying the braid-ends together, the great rib is split in three and the middle section thrown away. The two leaflet-bearing strips are bent in half and the basket pressed down in the middle to change the shape from triangular to a rounded, somewhat pendent one. In the cities isu are used for holding produce in markets, and in the countryside they are carried dangling from the ends of a pole slung over the shoulders of men returning from bush gardens. Dry isu are discarded or used for trash. This style is not used elsewhere in Polynesia but has been noted in Vanuatu, Fiji's neighbor to the west. Other quickly made baskets intended for short-term use are a split-rib with continuous rectangular sides (figure 1), and a large single-strip with keel bottom (color plate 8), both generally called *ketekete.* The split-rib basket is used for carrying small loads such as books or lunch to school, and the single-strip for carrying large amounts of food from the bush or market.

The most popular women's basket is the oval, keel-bottomed *kato* (figure 9) that is carried rucksack style on the backs of women transporting food from the bush. Kato with somewhat more flattened bottoms can be used for storage. According to region, kato are called instead ketekete, *tidre,* or *tabe* (pronounced tambe). Varying only in details, this basket has been made throughout central Polynesia.

Nearly as ubiquitous in Fiji is the *noke,* also known as *seci* (pronounced sethi). It is a small women's basket tied around the waist and used for collecting fish and shellfish. Shapes for the noke can vary from flat with a straight bottom and semicircular top edge (figure 10) to a deep, pouchlike shape with only slightly curved top (figure 11). Baskets having these configurations are peculiar to Fiji. As far as the Cook Islands to the east

and at least Vanuatu to the west, small versions of the kato were used instead for women's fishing baskets. I saw only one of this type in Fiji, in Vanua Levu (color plate 5).

Less used now is the squat, cylindrical *sova* (figure 12), sometimes called tabe. It is used for storing such items as clothes, babies' diapers, or weaving materials and implements. A nearly identical basket was formerly made in Samoa and Kapingamarangi. Other cylindrical coconut frond baskets but with a different bottom closing are made on the islands of Ovalau and Vanua Levu and in the Cook Islands.

Except for the bottom closing, all the above multistrip baskets are woven in a similar manner. First, the two or four long strips bearing the folded, narrowed leaflets are combined, then the great rib ends are brought together to form a hoop. Next, the sides are woven in twills of various kinds, and finally the bottom is closed. Control of the width of the leaves while plaiting and the method of connecting the leaflet tips determine the final shape of a basket.

French braid combinations produce the keel-bottomed kato. If the kato is finished with two French braids, a braid will be clearly visible on the inside and the outside will present a smooth surface (figure 8, right). If the initial group of leaflets is crossed before braiding, the inside will be smooth. If the strips of the second group are crossed before braiding, a braid will be clearly visible on the outside. Braiding by adding two parallel strips at a time will cause the keel to curve sharply, as does dropping accumulated leaflets from the French braid (figure 9). Another variation common in Vanua Levu requires five steps to close the bottom. The first strips are crossed, then French braided. The second set of strips covers the first braid in a band of check plaiting about 7 cm wide. The rows of strips extending out from both sides of this plaiting are closed into braids of the type normally used for finishing pandanus mats (figure 8, left).

The noke may be made from coconut leaflets that have been finely stripped with midribs removed, or not, or from the new white fronds with the fragile leaflets divided in half along the still-tender midribs. Continuous thinning and doubling up of the strips while plaiting narrows the cylinder. In the center where the leaflets converge, they are bound into two braids and a disklike shape is created. This is folded and bound in

Interior of a chief's house as seen by A. T. Agate and published in Wilkes' *Narrative.* Note the baskets lying on the floor and hanging on walls and in rafters. *Photo courtesy of Bishop Museum.*

half to result in a somewhat flat semicircular container (figure 10). Pulling together the not-yet-closed bottom of a modified cylinder, then braiding, will create a basket with a poofy shape once the rim is bound closed (figure 6). Nokes are always tied nearly closed at the top so that the newly caught fish, shrimp, or crabs cannot get out. The center opening is additionally protected by a covering of fresh green coconut leaflets (figure 11).

The sova, or tabe (figure 12), usually has its bottom edge defined by a ridge formed by slipping each outer-group leaflet of the unfinished cylinder behind the next. Plaiting then continues normally until the circular opening is nearly closed. Finally, in the center, two or four braids bind the ends securely. All are pulled inside and tied together or tucked through the plaiting. An alternative method closes the bottom with two French braids and results in an oval-shaped basket.

The top edge of a finished basket is sometimes covered with a strip of coconut fiber (figure 7) or, more often, either natural or organically dyed black pandanus is held in place by a 2-ply string of hibiscus inner bark (vau) (figure 10). When a strap is needed, it is braided with either pandanus or vau.

Despite the seeming ubiquity of coconut frond baskets, on closer inspection it turns out that the finer ones are not being made everywhere. They come primarily from the more traditional villages and the basket makers generally are older women. They make their baskets for themselves or, on request, as gifts for the younger women of their own village and as barter items for those of neighboring villages. Occasionally, baskets also turn up in markets for sale. Slowly, however, locally made baskets of leaf and vine are being supplanted by plastic bags and mold-made plastic baskets, all imported from abroad.

Once people move from traditional agrarian villages to the less communal towns, the opportunity and importance of passing on the old crafts decreases. In the new environment, fine coconut work baskets are no longer needed. The art of pandanus (voivoi) weaving, however, persists and evolves, as it is taught in schools and shared in women's groups. Members of a club may belong to the same church or share a common origin. Stylistic differences in the work of these groups have developed just as they might have in the past between villages or regions.

Pandanus baskets are produced by a thriving cottage industry, supplying objects for the urban Fijian and overseas tourist alike. Fine craftsmanship and the marriage of traditional forms and modern tastes have resulted in voivoi baskets with continuing wide appeal. The finest work in all Fiji is found in the Suva market, for sale. Shapes and patterns have changed somewhat over the years in response to consumer preferences. Current favorites in Suva are double-wall plaited containers of various sizes and shapes designed to be used as portfolios (figure 14), purses (figures 15, 16), travel or shopping bags (figure, page 96), or for laundry or storage. All are done in finely twilled and figured patterns over a layer of coarse check weave. The outer layer is executed in natural tan leaf and accented with natural brown (paogo, pronounced paongo) and dyed black (somo) strips. Larger plaited baskets are interlined with cardboard or, more often, split bamboo.

Another current favorite is the coil market basket. A good many of those sold in Suva's market are made by first- and second-generation Tuvalu women. Although they refer to these as Tongan-style baskets, the knot they use is the single-faced Samoan version.

Other plants with good basket-making properties (flexible when fresh and strong and durable when dry)

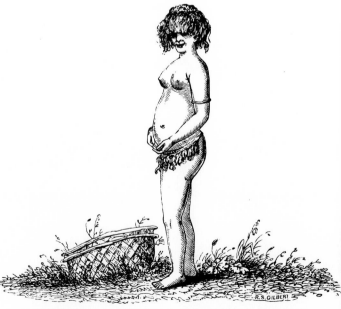

"Feejee Girl," from Wilkes' *Narrative. Photo courtesy of Bishop Museum.*

Figure 6. **Noke. Fiji.**
Traditional women's fishing basket made from a young
coconut frond with the leaflet midribs removed. The tie
and plaited rim are both of pandanus.
48 cm wide × 22 cm high

have been used in the regions where they grow. Frey-cinetia (most commonly called *wamere, wame,* and *mere* according to locale) is still used on Viti Levu and Vanua Levu to make fish-collecting baskets and other types of containers (figure, page 113). Where the forest habitats have given way to pasture and farmland, weavers now have to hike longer distances to gather the raw materials. Needless to say, this dampens their enthusiasm. In the forests of the eastern coastal area of Viti Levu, the bush climber *Flagellaria indica* (known by region as *qalo, wasila, walaki,* or *vere*) is actively used to make squat cylindrical storage baskets (figure 13) and small flat women's fishing baskets (figure, page 113). Both are executed from the split slender stems in the same 3-strand lattice work as is used in the freycinetia baskets. Many other lianas are used for making baskets, but a problem exists in identifying them from names given by informants. John W. Parham, in his *Plants of Fiji Islands,* wrote that "the same plant may have several names—or the same name may be used in different localities for different plants often belonging to distinct genera and families."

Containers of split mangrove aerial root (called *dogo,* pronounced ndongo) used to be made to protect and dispense the pillars of salt farmed on tidal flats of Viti Levu's arid western coasts. Those were traded to the interior and to nearby islands. Once salt was imported and sold cheaply in stores in the latter half of this century, the industry died.

Bamboo, while found throughout the wetter areas of the larger islands, is rarely used for making baskets today.

I was told that women used to catch fish in small (40-cm-diameter) traps, but they rarely do so now. On the southern island of Kadavu, a twined trap *(kawa)* (figure 5) was made for me from a combination of two beach creepers *(tokutolu* and *tuva).* The first woman's fish trap made there in some time, it looked just like the much larger (1-meter-diameter) ones made and used only by men. Those are still in use there and are conspicuously stored alongside houses of many of the coastal villages. Fish traps of the same technique and shape have been collected for the Bishop Museum from Rotuma and Samoa.

There is almost no early literature on Fijian baskets. Early writers mention without great elaboration that baskets are made of coconut, freycinetia, and rush. Members of the United States Exploring Expedition in 1840 collected two coconut frond baskets of types that are still made today: a split-rib basket and a *noke*—both pictured in their report (figures, pages 22 and 97). They also brought back twenty flat pandanus baskets and depicted small-mouthed box-shaped ones. The large flat (about 80 cm long) baskets that they found in maritime Fiji are indistinguishable from those collected from nearby Ha'apai, Tonga, by others at about the same time (figure 17). The black-and-tan patterns had a lively random quality within a geometric framework. That mix of very fine geometric patterns is not seen today, nor is the technique which requires weft strips to be inserted through slit warps. The boxlike baskets, in common with Tongan baskets of that time, had such characteristics as double walls with finer strips on the outside, no seams, right-angled weaving (that is, with strips that are woven parallel to the sides), and a top surface with a kind of trap-door lid in the center. Box shapes continue to be made but they are taller and lack the wide horizontal rim. Other new features include pandanus-whipped edges, 4-ply round handles, and plaiting extended from the top of the back surface to create a lid that covers just the top (figure 16) or continues partly down the front (figure, page 109).

Figure 7. **Purse. Vanua Levu, Fiji.**
Contemporary coconut leaf purse in the kato shape used
by Fijian women. The leaflets are split and woven separately from their midribs. The top edge is covered with
coconut fiber. Binding and strap are hibiscus inner bark.
19 and 33 cm wide × 26 cm high
Opposite page: Detail of bottom of purse.

Figure 8. **Two kinds of finishing braids for keel-bottomed baskets.**
Left: Kato matalalai. Macuata, Vanua Levu, Fiji. The second course is a 3-cm-wide plaited band. The strips extending from its sides are collected into the type of braid normally used for finishing pandanus mats.
Right: Tidre saitava. Bua, Vanua Levu, Fiji. 3-ply French braid of the most common type.

Figure 9. **Kato. Viti Levu, Fiji.**
A traditional women's 4-strip coconut leaf carrying
basket from Nadroumai, in southwestern Viti Levu. The
carrying straps are made of pandanus fiber. The graceful
bottom is achieved by doubling up the weaving strips
about 10 cm before the bottom braid. The braid is made
to arch sharply by keeping the number of strips carried in
the braid constantly low.
46 × 30.5 cm wide × 28 cm high

Figure 10. **Noke. Vanua Levu, Fiji.**
Traditional women's coconut leaf fishing basket from
the village of Sawani. The pandanus shoulder strap is a
modern feature added so that the noke may be used as
a purse.
45 cm wide × 21 cm high

Figure 11. **Noke. Vanua Levu, Fiji.**
Traditional women's fishing basket made in the village
of Vakativa. The fresh coconut leaflets across the top
opening are used to stop newly caught fish or crabs
from escaping.
37 cm wide × 21 cm high

Figure 12. **Tabe. Viti Levu, Fiji.**
A traditional 4-strip coconut leaf storage basket from
Nadroumai. The ridge near the top edge is distinctive of
the village, as is the finishing technique of removing all
leaf material from the midribs of the two finishing braids
that close the center bottom.
43 cm diameter × 20 cm high

Figure 13. **Sova. Viti Levu, Fiji.**
Traditional storage basket of vere from Savu, in coastal
southeastern Viti Levu, that is made with the 3-strand
lattice-work technique and reinforced by plaiting along
the rim. This hexagonal pattern is found in the Pacific
basin only as far east as Fiji.
43 cm diameter × 23 cm high

Figure 14. **Contemporary pandanus satchel. Fiji.**
This satchel is worked in two tones of leaf on the outside
and a coarser, one-color check weave inside.
36 cm wide × 44 cm high

Figure 15. **Pandanus purses. Fiji.**
These contemporary double-walled baskets purchased
in Suva in 1987 are worked in natural white and vegetal-
dyed black leaf. The coarser inside layer is plaited first,
then additional strips are tucked through the bottom
before being stripped finer to plait the otherwise separate
outside layer.
27 cm wide × 23 cm high, 31 cm wide × 32 cm high,
25 cm wide × 28 cm high

Figure 16. **Modern pandanus purse. Fiji.**
This modern black-and-white purse is plaited with
3-mm-wide strips of pandanus, lined in check weave
with 35-mm-wide strips, and stiffened with strips of
bamboo. This shape was originally devised for carrying
Bibles.
23 cm long × 13 cm wide × 26 cm high

Figure 17. **Mid-nineteenth-century pandanus satchel.**
Double-layered satchels of this type were woven
throughout the nineteenth century at least. They have
been collected both from Fiji and from nearby Ha'apai,
Tonga. Note that the horizontals in the fine patterns have
been inserted through the slitted verticals.
86 cm wide × 36.5 cm high

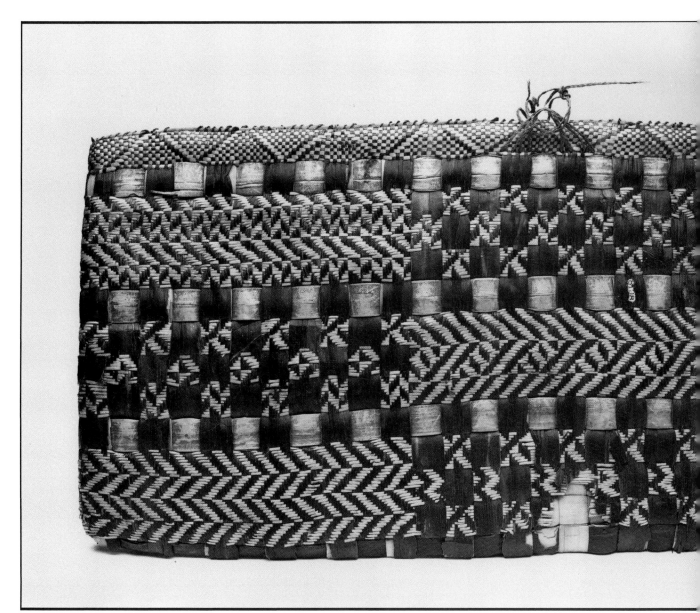

··TONGA··

The Kingdom of Tonga consists of three main island groups. Most people reside on the large flat southern island of Tongatapu where the capital, Nuku-'alofa, is located. About 270 kilometers north, the high island of Vava'u with nine neighbor islands and numerous islets compose the Vava'u Group. Least populous is the archipelago of the Ha'apai Group, with more than fifty tiny islands scattered about halfway between the two anchor groups.

Traditional fiber crafts are still very much alive in Tonga. Mat and tapa making, especially, are activities evident everywhere. Knowledge from these crafts carries over to the industry of basket making, which is practiced mostly for the tourist market. It is in Tongatapu and Vava'u that most of the pandanus baskets are made, especially in the villages close to the northern capital of Neiafu.

I was able to get to most of those weaving villages on local buses—largely open-sided vehicles that swing across causeway and copra plantation to the beat of reggae and inspirational Christian music. In villages the air rings with the sounds of the beating of tapa early in the day and the pounding of kava later on.

After tending to their main household duties of cooking, cleaning, and tending of kitchen gardens, most women spend the rest of the day plaiting. They work separately or together in their living rooms or community houses, weaving pandanus mats and baskets. Those working in groups divert themselves in friendly gossip, lively songs, and extemporaneous dances of a spirited nature.

Since every village has a number of bilingual women, I had no trouble finding translators. As my guide and I wandered from house to house and dropped in on the weavers, I learned that most had learned mat making at home and basket making in school. They use the mats themselves, but almost never the baskets. I wondered how this came to be, since collections by both Cook and Wilkes of beautiful fine pandanus objects indicated that they had been part of the culture for some time. Eventually I found some older women who told me that in the 1920s and

1930s the art had nearly died. Just before that time, the far-sighted Queen Salote perceived that the growing tourist industry could be a source of income for village women if they learned to make the items that the visitors wanted to buy. Toward that end she brought the kingdom's best weavers to her newly founded college in Nuku'alofa to teach young girls to make pandanus baskets. Those girls later went back to their villages and taught others. Those pandanus baskets, developed as a response to foreign requirements, were regarded only as an exchange for cash and were never adopted for local use.

Villages along the routes of the touring steamships, especially those near Nuku'alofa and Neiafu, developed bustling cottage industries. Villagers would greet tourists either on shore or along the ship's side to sell their handicrafts. This activity continued until recent decades when fewer ships have plied Tonga's waters. Then production slowed until the 1980s when more tourists began to arrive because of an increase in the number of air flights and of small boats passing through Neiafu's famous hurricane-proof harbor.

The flourishing basket industry affects more than village economies. It has contributed to stabilizing and reinforcing women's interrelationships, since women often gather together to plait and teach each other. A result of this kind of collaboration is the development of village and regional styles.

Most plaited baskets from Vava'u are executed in the check pattern and embellished by surface decoration. A currently popular style is said to have originated from the sewing technique called smocking and carries that name (figure 24). In smocking an introduced contrasting strip binds the check weave tightly into a repeating geometric pattern. A similar technique that does not pull on the strips it crosses is used in Tahiti and the southern Cook islands of Mangaia and Atiu.

Ha'apai, reknowned for its figured twill mats, produces baskets that carry black-and-tan patterns like those in the mats (figures 18, 20). On Tongatapu similar patterns in brown and tan cover the bottoms of trays (figure 21) and market baskets (figure 22), and the sides

Top left, A woman with newly made kato alu. *Top right,* Hundred-year-old coconut frond basket trimmed with sennit cord and bamboo stick. *Bottom left,* Placing the upper surface of prepared kie tonga type of pandanus into rolls. *Bottom right,* 'Utulei, Vava'u, artisan and her nearly finished laundry basket of pandanus strips coiled over mangrove aerial root.

of satchels (figure 24). In nearby Fiji, its Lau Group a short sail west of Tonga's Ha'apai Group and its people connected to Tonga through generations of marriage, finely woven baskets and purses sport similar black-and-tan patterns.

Flat rectangular pandanus baskets collected by Wilkes and others in the nineteenth century from Tonga (usually Ha'apai) and Fiji are indistinguishable from each other (figure 17). These baskets, said to have been used for fishing, have double walls with the finer outer plaiting characterized by having quarter-centimeter strips inserted through slits that create the intricate black-and-tan geometric patterns. This technique is now obsolete.

Another antecedent to modern basket styles is the boxlike plaited pandanus basket that formed a part of both Cook's and Wilkes' Tonga collections. They are quite similar to Fijian specimens collected by Wilkes in their double-wall construction, right-angle plaiting with geometric patterns in brown or black and tan, lack of seams, top openings defined by horizontal lips on all four sides, and, in Tonga only, on two opposite sides. In W. C. McKern's unpublished manuscript on the material culture of Tonga in the early 1920s similar baskets are mentioned. One was made without the older optional flap lid and another had a new kind of lid that sat like a little pill-box hat on a short vertical lip around the small mouth. Neither of these is made today and must have been going out of style at that time.

A recent technique seen only in Tonga uses kako, a particular kind of pandanus braid. In the 1960s baskets were solidly covered with kako. This is now giving way to a modification that uses the kako only as a trim (figure 23).

A genre new to Tonga in this century is the pandanus coil basket. It is always made with the double-face knot. Vava'u specialties include small oval containers with lids, circular 1-meter-tall lidded clothes baskets (kato 'uli) (figures 25, 26), and large circular trays (figure 27). All are made with triangle-based designs in tan, brown, and black. Other favorites, seen more commonly in the south, serve as shopping (figures 28, 30) and storage baskets and purses (figure 29). In only one village is another core material substituted for the coconut leaf midribs that are generally used. In the Vava'u village of 'Utulei, mangrove aerial root is

used because it is faster to prepare and is better suited for the large four- and six-sided baskets made there.

There are no pandanus coil baskets in early collections, and McKern, writing in the early 1920s, makes no mention of them. I was told by various elderly informants that the basket was first made in Tonga in the mid-1920s at Queen Salote's newly opened college in Nuku'alofa. Others believed it to have been introduced by the wives of Niue construction workers brought to Tonga by King Tupou II. The original head tutor of the Queen's college remembers that the knotting technique was devised by some students who were experimenting with variations on the knot used in making the ceremonial kato alu. They wanted to use pandanus for this class project but considered it inappropriate for a pandanus basket to have the same knot as that used for the ceremonial alu one. Perhaps the students were inspired by those Niue models.

The ceremonial basket (figure 31), made from the tough *Epipremnum pinnatum* vine called alu in Tonga, was collected by Captain Cook and is still made today. A coil basket made only in the single-face knotting technique, its sole use was as a container for the small fine mat–wrapped gourds called fangu that contain handmade, scented coconut oil. Today white tapa enfolds ornate glass bottles. The kato alu is given away at weddings, funerals, and births and then saved to be given away again. The most common shapes are round or oval with somewhat bulging sides. The long side generally varies from 30 cm to 1 meter, but special ones have been described as up to nearly 2 meters. The rectangular types collected by Cook have not been made in this century. A finished basket is traditionally colored black, usually by a solution of soot from burned candlenuts (tuitui; *Aleurites moluccana*) and raw inner bark liquid from koka (*Bischofia javanica*), then sometimes decorated with undyed braided coconut fiber or, in the past, shells. Few kato alu are made today. Difficulty of working with the stiff material is one reason. Increasing scarcity of alu is another. Most alu today is gathered from the island of 'Eua and brought to Nuku'alofa and Neiafu for sale. The revival of the art on Tongatapu has taken an ironic turn. One woman has recently begun to offer alu baskets for sale. However, it would seem that she was previously a worker of pandanus only, for her traditional-appearing baskets sport

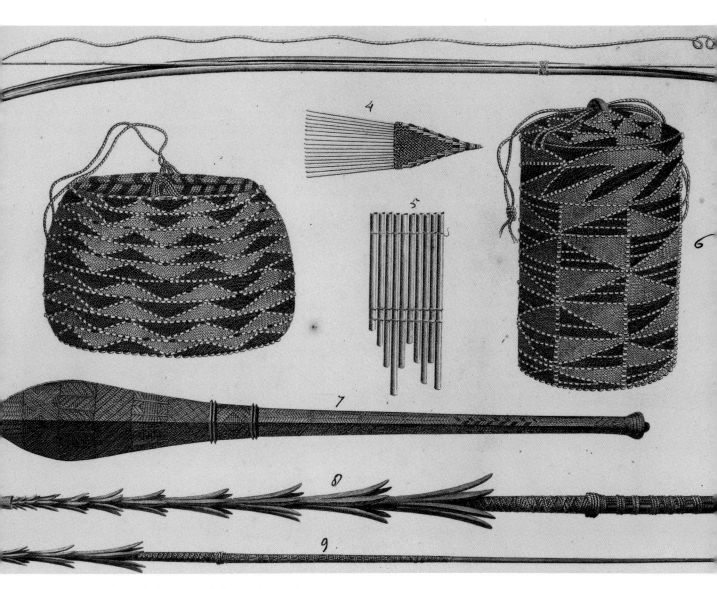

Two coconut fiber baskets (mosikaka) as depicted in
Cook's *Voyage Towards the South Pole and Round the
World.* Original drawing by Chapman. *Photo courtesy of
Bishop Museum.*

the new two-faced knot. They further depart from tradition by not being dyed black. Despite these liberties, her product has been enthusiastically received by Tongans needing ceremonial baskets.

In the years 1920 and 1921 McKern found both temporary and permanent coconut frond baskets in everyday use. By 1987 only the full-leaf baskets were actively used. Two that were conspicuous in markets when green and in trash piles when brown were the open-sided split-rib *pola* and the single-strip keel-bottom *kato polopola* (color plate 8). Both were used for carrying produce from the field and market. In Vava'u I observed two old-style baskets that used to be common but are rarely seen today. One is given to those who attend funerals; called *kato fakaloumasi*, it is a small split-rib basket with braids along both sides of its pointed bottom. The other, called *'oa*, is a small check-weave, 2-strip basket made in a variety of shapes and used today as a purse (figure 32). Coconut frond baskets no longer seen are the more finely made *'oa* that was made in twilled patterns and the much larger open-leaf baskets used to carry food and gifts. See the table on page 42 for a descriptive listing of Tongan coconut frond baskets that were recorded in the twentieth century.

Some other baskets collected by Cook have completely passed from use. Flexible, knotted sennit satchels continued to be made through the nineteenth century. The two collected in the late 1800s and now housed at the small museum at Tupou College just outside Nuku'alofa are labeled as having been used for fishing. They are called *kato kafa* (sennit basket). The same type of sachel has been observed in Samoa and Tahiti. Sennit baskets made in the coil technique perhaps went out of use sooner, as they do not appear in later published collections.

The finest basket ever found in Polynesia is the *mosikaka*. It was prominent in Cook's collections (figure, page 49), but within sixty years it had declined to such an extent that Wilkes' crew could obtain only one. It was not even remembered by those interviewed by McKern in the early 1920s. The mosikaka was made from the dyed and undyed separated fibers of coconut husk, leaf sheath, or roots (information is conflicting on this detail). The single strands were twined together in double pairs to create a flat, flexible satchel. (See Mafi 1986, for diagrams.) They were also constructed on bases of knotted sennit, or checkerwork pandanus, or wooden cylinders, and (a variant technique) on coconuts. Frequently its triangular patterns were accented with small white shells. One early writing states that the soft mosikaka was used by chiefly ladies to carry bits of white tapa impregnated with fragrant coconut oil. As for other uses of the mosikaka, we can only hope that some lost document will come to light with descriptions of the way of life in eighteenth-century Tonga and the part that baskets played in it.

Figure 18. **Pandanus purse. Ha'apai, Tonga.**
This new-shape basket is plaited in a traditional pattern.
It is woven with 4-mm strips, lined in 2-cm-wide check
weave, and interlined with cardboard.
26-cm side × 26-cm side × 8 cm deep

Tongan Coconut Frond Baskets

Type	Description	Name	Use
Split-rib	separate rectangular sides, 2-course French braid closing	kato pola	carrying long root crops
	same	kato fakaha'atu'ia	taking cooked food to the king
	with 2 handles	kato kai tunu	transporting food to workers
	pointed bottom defined by two French braids	kato fakaloumasi	given filled with food to attendants at funerals
Single-strip, keel bottom	generic name current name	kato lou niu polopola	carrying food from the bush, often on poles made from the coconut great rib
	with hau handles	kato ha'amo	
	small and deep	kato tuki	holding Tongan medicine
	very large—end halves of basket made separately then lashed together carried on 1 pole by 2 men carried on 2 poles by 4 men	kato fakahunga kato umuhula	presenting a huge pig to the chief at special ceremonies
Multiple-strip (2 or 4), keel closing	check or twill double outside keel braid sometimes has handles sometimes decorated with shells and fine sennit	'oa fakaono	in the past for holding the clothes of a noble's daughter while she bathes
	same but smaller and finer	'oa	as a fishing basket holding plaiting and tapa implements holding special things such as fragrant oils
	leaflets stripped from midribs and woven separately decorated with fine sennit outside braid protected by a strip of bamboo	kato tu'a niu	

Sources: McKern 192–, Mafi 1986, Koch 1955, Tupou College collection, and personal observation.

Figure 19. **Coconut leaf purse. Niuatoputapu, Tonga.**
This modern version of a traditional basket is made from
two coconut strips. Leaflet material is separated from the
midribs in order to plait each separately.
36 cm wide × 21 cm high

Figure 20. **Pandanus satchel. Ha'apai, Tonga.**
Front surface of a large (30 cm wide × 49 cm high) flat
satchel that is worked in shades of undyed leaf. The
inside has two sections separated by a check-woven
panel and the outside has another full-size pocket. The
multi-pocketed form is believed to be traditional.
Opposite page. Top: surface revealed by lifting flap
Bottom: back surface

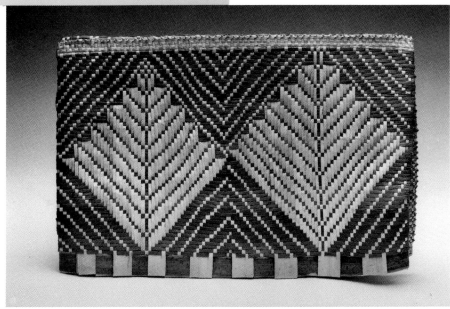

Figure 21. **Contemporary trays. Tongatapu, Tonga.**
The market and craft shops in Nuku'alofa brim with trays plaited in what seems an endless variety of patterns. The mat work is mounted on masonite or plywood and bordered by two rows of double-face coil knotting. These trays range in size from 24 to 48 cm in length.

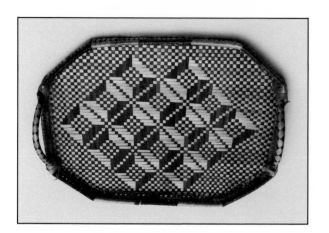

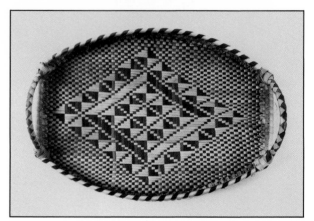

Figure 22. **Coil market basket. Tongatapu.**
Worked in natural tan, brown, and dyed black, this basket combines the coil and plaiting techniques. The bottom is a sandwich of pandanus between layers of pandanus plaiting.
40 cm long × 32 cm wide × 23 cm high

Figure 23. **Pandanus purses. Tongatapu, Tonga.**
All these purses, made expressly for sale, have three
layers: tapa lining, cardboard interlining, and braided
pandanus outer surface.
*They range in size from 3.5 cm wide × 9 cm high to 23 cm
long × 12 cm wide × 19.5 cm high*

Figure 24. **Pandanus book bags. Tonga.**
The three layers—coarsely woven pandanus, interlining
of cardboard, and fine plaited outside surface—are often
sewn together on treadle sewing machines before being
assembled with pandanus whip-stitching. The basket on
the left has rows of smocking.
*38 cm long × 17 cm wide × 28 cm high, 44 cm long ×
21 cm wide × 36 cm high*

Figure 25. **Pandanus coil clothes basket. Vava'u, Tonga.**
An 80-cm-high contemporary basket with natural tan
and brown pandanus strips wound on bundles of coconut leaf midribs.

Figure 26. **Pandanus coil clothes baskets. Tonga.**
The front basket is from Tongatapu and the pair in the
rear from Vava'u.
Heights vary from 70 to 90 cm

Figure 27. **Contemporary tray. Vava'u, Tonga.**
Pandanus strips wrapped around a core of coconut
leaflet midribs create this 49-cm-wide tray from the
village of Talihau.

Figure 28. **Pandanus coil basket. Vava'u, Tonga.**
Worked in natural tan and brown leaflet wrapped
around coconut leaf midribs, this type of basket is made
for sale and is rarely used by Tongan women.
32 cm wide

Figure 29. **Pandanus coil basket. Tongatapu, Tonga.**
A 20-cm-high contemporary basket purchased in
Nuku'alofa market. The slit work and long wraps are
distinctive features rarely seen elsewhere in Tonga.

Figure 30. **Pandanus coil market basket.
Tongatapu, Tonga.**
This basket shape is said to be a response to the preferences of New Zealand women. The graceful integration of handles with basket rim is unusual.
Basket part measures 43 cm long × 26 cm wide × 13 cm high

Figure 32. **'Oa. Vava'u, Tonga.**
These 'oa were all in use as purses when purchased from women on the island of Vava'u. These 2-strip coconut leaf baskets exhibit the diversity of 'oa shapes. The 'oa on the left has a flat oval bottom with a double braid running down the center; the middle basket has a double-braid keel bottom; and the third has a 4-corner flat check bottom. 'Oa are now passing from use.
27 cm long × 24.5 cm wide × 19 cm high, 39 cm wide × 21 cm high, 33 cm long × 22 cm wide × 18 cm high

Figure 31. **Kato alu. Tonga.** *Opposite page.*
This type of ceremonial basket, first collected by Cook, is still made and used. The rounded shape shown is the most common seen today. The basket is decorated with sennit and covered with a black sooty mud.
29 and 25.5 cm diameter × 22 cm high

Vava'u woman with 'oa purse

··SAMOA··

To my Western eyes the countryside of Upolu, Western Samoa, looks like one endless parkland. Situated in carefully tended landscaped surroundings, the traditional open-sided oval houses called *fale* appear nearly like large kiosks or bandstands, made distinctive by the overlapping plaited panels of coconut frond hung from the eaves. These 2-meter-long, 2-strip panels called *pola sisi* can be lowered to protect the interior from the elements. They are woven in a variety of twill combinations that are the same as those incorporated in the fishing, carrying, and storage baskets that were once so common.

The coconut leaf baskets actively made in Western Samoa today are of the single-strip temporary sort. One has a double-braid keel bottom (color plate 8). The other has a flat bottom, its squat cylindrical shape caused by the way its closing braid runs around the lower edge of the cylinder and then down the center of the bottom (figure 33). This closure creates a larger basket from the same size strip. In the 1920s, when he was in Samoa, Sir Peter Buck was told that this basket originally came from Niue. In recent times it has turned up in Fiji, Tuvalu, and Tokelau, but it is believed in all those places that the style was introduced from Samoa.

On most other islands of Polynesia, each type of basket has its own name, and sometimes many different baskets share a name. But in Samoa there is the unusual practice of giving the two most common baskets various names. One, the keel-bottom basket (color plate 8) can be called *'ato fili tasi* (1-braid basket) or *'ato fili lua* (2-braid basket) according to the interpretation of the number of braids used to close the bottom. But it is also termed *'ato mata* or *'ato 'ato* depending on whether it is green or dry. The most common name, however, is *'ato fu'e umu* since it is most often employed in receiving food freshly cooked from the *umu* (earth oven).

The other common basket (figure 33) with several names was known to Buck as *'ato fili tolu* (3-braid basket), which describes the apparent number of braids used to close the bottom (reminiscent of the two halves of a circle and its diameter), and *'ato fa'aniuē* (Niue-style basket), referring to the island of its believed origin. However, its chief name is *'ato toli 'ulu,* since its primary use is in bringing breadfruit (*'ulu*) or other food crops that have been picked (*toli*) to the village.

More durable coconut frond baskets are called *ola.* In 1920 Buck found the following baskets in use daily. *Ola malū* (soft basket; figure 37), plaited in check weave and closed with two braids into a keel bottom, was worn at the small of the back while tied about the waist. Women used it while collecting fish and shellfish in the lagoon. It was made from one or two thinned great-rib strips with the leaflets split in half and the midribs removed. The *ola tū* (firm basket), woven from two strips, had horizontal twill plaiting and a 2-braid keel bottom. This larger and stronger basket was used by women catching fish driven from hiding places in the lagoon. Buck also saw the similar but smaller and more elaborately made *si'u ola* (figure 37) used for collecting freshly caught fish (*si'u* is a kind of fish). These fishing baskets are still used in Western Samoa but not as much as in the past. The generic names *ola fāgota* (fishing basket), *malū,* and *malū fāgota* are now used interchangeably by the younger generation to describe the various sorts of fishing baskets. New uses of the ola

'Ato in use in Apia market

58

Figure 33. **3-braid full-leaf coconut leaf basket.
Western Samoa.**
A traditional basket still very much in use today. The
circular bottom closure results in a basket capable of
carrying a greater volume than a keel basket made from
the same length strip.
60 cm long × 35 cm wide × 32 cm high

are as school book bags or, with the addition of a lining, as purses.

Similar to these baskets but more intricately made is the 2-strip, vertical-twill 'ato 'afa (figure 35), once used for holding the coconut-fiber cording ('afa) belonging to a chief. It is distinguished by a handsome, complex, 5-strand keel braid that is unusual in the way the strips drop out of the braid and then return to it. In the Bishop Museum collection only one other basket appears to carry this same closing. It was collected by Kenneth P. Emory in 1931 from Napuka in the Tuamotu Archipelago.

Twilled cylindrical 2-strip baskets once made throughout Samoa are less common today. Buck knew this squat coconut basket as 'ato lavalava (figure 36), which described its use for storing the wrap garment known as lavalava. He wondered if this round basket was an introduced form. It is similar in shape, manufacture, and use to the Fijian sova ni sulu (sulu is the Fijian word for lavalava). Today, the basket is referred to as ola lāpotopoto (round basket) and is used for holding laundry. The most common technique of closing the bottom begins with forming a twist at what will be the lower edge of the cylinder. This changes the weaving plane to the horizontal. In what seems to be the most common method of finishing, the naturally narrowing leaflets allow the bottom to close up as the weaving proceeds. Leaflets are gathered into four braids, which are inserted back through the weaving. As in Fiji, a lid once said to be made to close the container is no longer in use.

Unfortunately, because pandanus baskets were not collected from Samoa until long after first European contact, nothing is known of earlier styles. The pieces collected ·in the nineteenth century for the Bishop Museum were small, rigid, boxy, and with one or two openings bordered by a horizontal lip (figure 34). They had double walls, checker weaving on the horizontal surfaces, and finer black-and-white patterns on the sides. Similar containers with single openings only were collected during the same period from Tonga and Fiji. A larger version called taga (pronounced tanga), was said to have been made for storing siapo (bark cloth), but no examples exist today. Small flat satchels woven in diagonal check weave collected in Samoa by Buck in the 1920s were believed by his informants to be a modern development. Baskets with similar characteristics were found throughout central Polynesia in the same decade.

Baskets made of half-cm-wide strips of pandanus coiled on a flat flexible core have been made in Samoa from at least the middle 1800s (figure 39). Characteristic of this basket is the use of the single-face knot and the open pattern created by the open spaces that result from extra wraps around the core bundle. The manufacture of coil baskets in Samoa has dwindled today to that of small, fairly flat versions (figure 40). The more common hot pads have knotted patterns that are distinctly related to the swirling star patterns favored a century ago.

Braided sennit cording was once used to make flat baskets in a kind of knotted netting technique. Although he could find no one who could make such a basket, in 1930 Buck was able to collect one on the island of Sawai'i that he was told had been in the family for generations, and another from the island of Ofu (figure 38). Containers of this type were used for holding fishhooks and line, and for holding carpenters' tools. Cook collected the same type of basket from Tonga, where it was made until at least 1900.

Fale in Western Samoa. *Photo by Carolyn Yacoe.*

Figure 34. **Nineteenth-century pandanus boxes. Samoa.**
Such double-section boxes appear to be unique to
Samoa. The dark strips are made from the outer layer of
the stem of the wild banana plant.
14.5 cm long × 14.5 cm wide × 10 cm high, 13.5 cm
long × 25.5 cm wide × 10 cm high, 13.5 cm long ×
25.5 cm wide × 10 cm high

Figure 35. **'Ato 'afa. Samoa.**
This 4-strip keel-bottom coconut frond basket was
already considered rare when it was collected in the
1920s. It was once used for holding a chief's coconut
fiber cording.
48.5 cm wide × 28 cm high

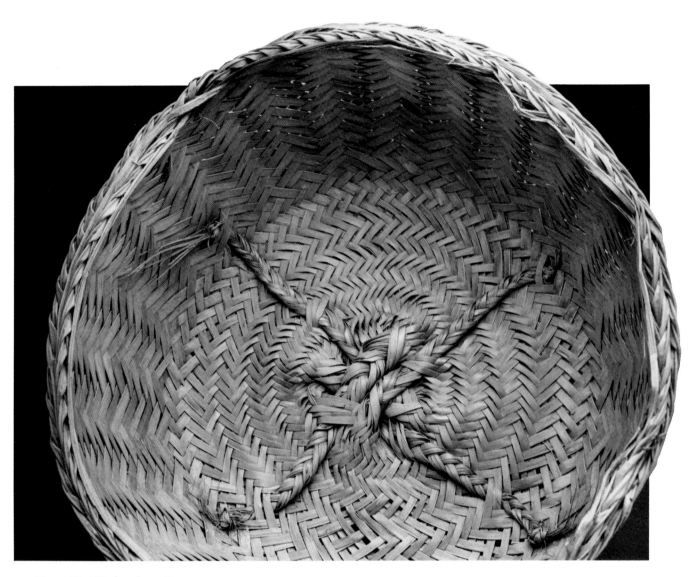

Figure 36. **'Ato lavalava. Samoa.**
A storage basket made in 1926. The inside, as seen here,
shows the four braids that bind up the converging coconut leaflet ends. This technique, now rare in Samoa, is
still common in Fiji today.
45 cm diameter × 22 cm high

Figure 37. **1920s coconut leaf fishing baskets. Samoa.**
Two kinds of si'u ola with an ola malū in front. The ola
malū has a soft smooth surface as a result of having been
plaited without midribs.
*Back to front: 43 and 30 cm wide × 32.5 cm high, 23 cm
wide × 31 cm high, 27 and 20 cm wide × 30 cm high*

Figure 38. **Traditional sennit satchel. Ofu, Samoa.**
This satchel was collected in 1930. It was used to store
fish hooks and line. Larger satchels were made to hold
carpenters' tools. Bags of this type have also been made
in Tonga and Tahiti.
27 and 23 cm wide × 15.5 cm high

Figure 39. **1927 pandanus coil basket. Samoa.**
Note that the pattern on the basket is repeated on the lid.
Modern Samoan hot pads carry this same design.
*Basket: 30 cm diameter × 13 cm high, lid: 30.5 cm
diameter × 2.5 cm high*

66

Figure 40. **Pandanus coil light cover. Western Samoa.**
The two sides are attached by means of buttons and
loops.
28 cm diameter × 15 cm deep

··COOK ISLANDS··

The Cook Islands extend across some 1,300 kilometers of ocean with nearly 1,000 kilometers separating the northern and southern groups. While both groups have about the same number of islands, the southern group, which includes the capital island of Rarotonga, has nearly 90 percent of the land and population. Although basket making continues to some extent in the rest of the Cook Islands, in Rarotonga it has just about ceased altogether.

"I never wanted to learn to weave when I was young. When my mother tried to teach me, I would run away to play." These were the words of one of the few older women on that island who could remember how to plait coconut fronds. Seated on her front door stoop with the green craggy interior mountain peaks rising behind her, she set to work. After a false start, she wove her first basket in years, a small split-rib that she had used as a child for carrying food and books to school (figure 1, right).

Temporary coconut frond baskets with split-rib top and French rolled or braided bottom are more actively made on the other southern islands. Women on the island of Mauke make small split-rib baskets for picking maile and large ones for carrying food from the garden. Other temporary baskets are made as well. The round 'ō'ini (figure 54) is still used today in the southern islands for collecting shellfish and in the north (where they are called tōngini) for carrying and holding food as it cooks in the umu. The rather rudimentary raurau and pite are also used in the north for umu cooking. Raurau are made somewhat flat and can be wrapped around food to be cooked. Pite, a kind of raurau with corners, has a pocketlike shape that holds the food more securely.

Throughout most of the Cook Islands, 2-strip keel baskets are made for carrying and fishing (figure 41). Round 2-strip flat-bottomed baskets closed with a 2-course French braid remain in use on the northern island of Manihiki for collecting shellfish and storing clothes. With the finishing touch of a pandanus-wrapped top edge, they are currently made and used by women in the southern group for purses and sewing

baskets (figure 42). The baskets are known as kete kīkau on Rarotonga and kete nīkau on Atiu. Except in Fiji, and in Tonga, Samoa, and Tokelau where it is rare, the flat-bottomed basket with 2-course closing is made only in the Cook Islands. While the temporary and permanent coconut frond baskets discussed above continue in use today, their manufacture has declined considerably in recent years since the younger generation of women has little interest in learning to weave.

In the 1930s ethnologists from the Bishop Museum made an exhaustive study of Cook Islands culture, including its baskets. From their observations, Sir Peter Buck concluded, "The advent of Western culture has not appreciably affected the need for these articles." The table on pages 74 and 75 shows the variety of coconut frond baskets seen at that time. The complicated and elaborately decorated kete ngahengahe (color plate 7) was made for Buck in 1930 by the only woman on Manihiki who could remember how to make it. That basket and the open-leaflet, U-shaped carrier believed an import from Tahiti are no longer made.

Since few baskets were systematically collected from the Cook Islands before this century, little is known of early styles, techniques, or uses. James Edge-Partington, in his book on objects in European museums in the 1890s, depicts a flat pandanus satchel from Rarotonga, finely plaited in diagonal twills with tiny geometric designs and serrated top edge. It was probably made like those collected in the early twentieth century (figure 46). All were begun at the top edge, plaited as a cuff, and closed at the bottom with multiple courses of plaiting (and in the 1930s with a machine-sewn seam). This is the same order followed as that used in making a keel-bottom coconut frond basket. The top edge was usually serrated, but sometimes it was level or finished with a French braid. Pandanus baskets with various sorts of braid-bottom closures have been found in Fiji, the Austral Islands, Tahiti, the Tuamotu Islands, Easter Island, and New Zealand, as well as Palau and Vanuatu.

A traditional pandanus satchel that was flat, plaited in check, and had a slip-on lid was called tuluma. It

Figure 41. **Pukapuka. Northern Cook Islands.**
This traditional 2-strip keel-bottom coconut frond basket
is often tied in the middle of the rim and carried by men
while fishing.
38 cm long × 26 cm wide × 25 cm high

was made small for storing fishhooks and large for *malo* (men's loincloth). Worked in a diagonal check weave with double strips, it was still made in the northern island of Pukapuka in the 1930s. New-style baskets made throughout the northern islands in 1930 were plaited in a diagonal check weave with geometric designs created by overlaying strips of red-dyed pandanus. Constructed with flat bottoms, they were plaited from the bottom up and had level top edges (figure 45). This type and the flat satchel with braided bottom are still made in the north for home use, but the material of choice is *rito* (see below).

Most pandanus baskets made for the tourist trade today are produced in the southern group. Frequently seen are boxlike purses with patterned right-angle plaiting that is gaily accented in overlaid synthetically dyed hau (color plate 6). The artisans prefer to make the baskets brightly colored rather than in natural tans despite the extra work involved and repeated requests from purchasers. Mangaia and Atiu also produce baskets that have brightly colored ribbons of artificial raffia threaded and twisted through the plaiting to add a textural dimension (figure 44). In contrast, baskets shaped much like modern flat shopping bags executed in a continuation of the old style of serrated top, diagonal plaiting, and wide-braid bottom closure today lack the geometric patterning favored earlier.

Coil baskets with pandanus wrapping were seen in the 1930s in Pukapuka, where they had been recently introduced from Samoa. At about the same time, a similar pandanus coil basket was seen in the Tuamotus by Kenneth P. Emory, who was told that it had been introduced late in the previous century from Manihiki. Whatever its history, the practice of this technique in the Cook Islands has not persisted.

A material especially favored in the north for trade baskets is rito, which is made from the top surface of the new, yet-unfolded coconut leaf. If the newly peeled strips are immediately placed in the sun to dry, a brown color results. If the strips are boiled before drying (again in the sun), the preferred brilliant white will result. The finest plaiting in Polynesia today is done in rito.

The practice of weaving rito, according to Buck, was imported from the Gilbert Islands to Rakahanga early in this century. It was rapidly adopted because of the beauty of the material and the similarity in handling to that of pandanus. Plaiting of hats and purses with the quarter-centimeter rito strips is still carried on in the northern Cook Islands. Use of this material never caught on among women who are native to the southern islands. In the 1920s the flat, twilled satchel was the popular shape. Most common now is the 12-cm-high lidded cylinder (figure 48) that is worked around a tin can. Identical ones have been made in the last twenty years in Tokelau. Rito is also combined with polished coconut shells (figure 43) and with large iridescent bivalve shells to fashion purses (figure 47), fans, and necklaces—all destined for sale to tourists. Women in the northern group today use rito to make small purses in the styles that used to be worked in pandanus in the 1920s. These are made for personal use only, since the stores in Rarotonga no longer order them. These small purses may be worked in white or brown rito and are sometimes decorated with embroidery of brightly dyed artificial raffia.

Most baskets made in the Cook Islands for sale are plaited of pandanus or rito. They are made on nearly every island except Rarotonga, where they are sold. They are sent there on the only means of cargo transport—the one ship that plies the waters between Samoa and the southernmost Cook island. Since arrivals are infrequent and the route varies with each trip, the selection of baskets available is generally limited to products of the islands most recently visited, and is best right after the (unscheduled) ship shows up. At another time of year a totally different selection may be available.

Figure 42. **Kete nīkau. Cook Islands.**
This modern adaptation of a traditional coconut basket is
used today as a purse by Rarotongan women. The top
edge is wrapped with pandanus strips.
Opposite page: the initial closing braid as seen from the
inside. *30 cm long × 26.5 cm wide × 15 cm high*

Basket-making activity for the tourist trade has decreased markedly of late. This is due not only to the unpredictable shipping service but also to the increased flow of cash from relatives in New Zealand and the lack of interest among the younger generation in learning the craft. In addition there is less need for cash on the outer islands because few consumer goods are sold there and most people grow a good part of their own food. Contributing to the decline in pandanus work in the southern islands was a mealybug infestation sometime after 1930 that devastated a good part of the pandanus groves, seriously crippling the plaiting industry there. Although trees are recovering now, the craft is only marginally being revived.

Figure 43. **Purse. Northern Cook Islands.**
Purse made of coconut shell, rito plaiting, and cowrie shells. Each rito strip is no more than 2 mm wide.
13 cm wide × 15 cm high

Figure 44. **Contemporary pandanus basket. Mangaia, southern Cook Islands.**
This basket is used by island women for carrying purchases, sewing, books, and personal effects. The heavily worked surface decoration of artificial raffia is unique to Mangaia and Atiu. *Basket courtesy of Dave Thompson.*
11.5 cm long × 5.5 cm wide × 8.5 cm high

Cook Island Coconut Frond Baskets—Northern Islands

Island	Type	Name	Use
Penrhyn (Tongareva)	French braid rim, joined sides, unsplit rib bottom	raurau	holding large articles of food
	2-strip basket, keel bottom; small	taunga	holding dried fish
	medium	kete	holding freshly cooked fish
	large	tupono	holding freshly caught fish
Manihiki and Rakahanga	leaflets from opposite strips plaited into various kinds of nearly flat shapes	raurau	food platters when flat cooking receptacle when rolled and tied around food to be cooked
	raurau with plaiting doubled on itself to create a pointed or 4-cornered enclosed form	pite	gathering and carrying shellfish cooking receptacle
	round 8-strip 'ō'ini	tōngini	
	single-frond in a U shape	none collected	
	2-strip basket with flat oval bottom and double French braid closing	kete	receptacle for food or miscellaneous items
	separate leaflets without midribs braided together, twilled, closed with a French braid combination, then decorated	kete ngahengahe	holding clothes
Pukapuka	similar to Manihiki raurau	laulau	serving food
	much like pite but more varied	angapilo	collecting shellfish and crabs
	angapilo with split leaflets	angapilo mulilua	collecting shellfish
	single-strip basket, keel closing	kete	carrying raw food
	2-strip basket, extra leaflets added, keel closing	ola	catching or holding fish
	rectangular 4-strip 'ō'ini	angapilo wai kave	children's fishing basket

Southern Islands

Island	Type	Name	Use
Aitutaki	2 kinds of nearly flat forms	raurau	food platter
	round 8-strip 'ō'ini	ohini	holding cooked foods
	split-rib basket with 1 braid, 2 braids, or braid and roll closing	all called tapora	food containers
	single-strip basket with 1- or 2-braid keel closing	tapora	carrying food
	4-strip basket, 3-stage keel closing	kete nīkau	
Mangaia	2-strip basket, keel closing	kete nīkau	
	large	kete rore	carrying cooked foods to feasts
	same	vai'ata	hung in house scaffolding to store cooked fish
	medium	kete takoto	carrying cooked foods and small fish
	small	kete 'apua / kete tautai	fisherman's basket worn tied around his waist
	split-rib basket, 1-braid keel closing	peru	carrying home uncooked food

Sources: Buck 1927, 1932 (no. 92), 1932 (no. 99), 1944; and Beaglehole 1938.

Figure 45. **Pandanus purses. Manihiki and Rakahanga, Cook Islands.**
The patterns in these 1930s trade purses are created by dark red strips inserted after the plaiting is complete.
Average size: 18 cm long × 4 cm wide × 15 cm high

Figure 46. **Pandanus satchels. Cook Islands.**
The satchel on the left has a red design; it was collected
from Atiu in 1930. The one on the right, found in 1920,
carries a dark brown pattern. Both have bottom closures;
that of the 1930 satchel is machine sewn, the 1920 one
plaited.
30 cm wide × 51 cm high, 24 cm wide × 47 cm high

Figure 47. **Rito purse. Northern Cook Islands.**
A purse woven in rito and decorated with shells. Modifi-
cations in the amount of plaiting can produce fans and
neck pieces. All are made expressly for sale. About 30
cm across.

Figure 48. **Rito containers. Northern Cook Islands.**
Contemporary rito cylinders, finely woven in variations
of the same zigzag pattern. The uniform basket shape
and size are achieved by plaiting over a tin can.
11 cm diameter × 12 cm high

··FRENCH POLYNESIA··

Five island groups make up the French overseas territory known as French Polynesia. Its some 120 islands and atolls, with a combined area of nearly 4,000 square kilometers, extend over four million square kilometers of ocean. Although this is an area equivalent to that of all the rest of central Polynesia, there does not seem to be an equivalent variety of contemporary basket forms. A far greater diversity may well have existed in pre-contact times, and is hinted at in dictionary listings of basket names, but we have no adequate record of it.

Little systematic collecting or describing of French Polynesian baskets occurred until early in this century when anthropologists from the Bishop Museum visited the major island groups of Polynesia. By that time investigators found that basket making was in serious decline. In 1923 Ralph Linton, in his "Material Culture of the Marquesas Islands," observed, "The twin arts of matting and basketry appear to have been less developed in the Marquesas than in any other part of tropical Polynesia and both have been nearly destroyed by European contact." He went on to note that "the manufacture of all but the simplest baskets had been discontinued in the Marquesas in 1920." Of the two coconut frond baskets he described, only one, the 'ō'ini, is still made today. Pandanus baskets were no longer being made. An example of an earlier style that Linton saw at the Peabody Museum in Salem, Massachusetts, is shaped like an envelope and is constructed of two layers of check plaiting with the finer layer on the inside.

In 1938 Buck wrote of Mangareva, "The plaiting craft has a local peculiarity in that coconut leaves were not used," and, "The old form of *pakete* [the general term for baskets] has been replaced by Tahitian and Tuamotu types both in coconut and pandanus." The enormous sacks with 3- and 4-ply French braid edge recorded by Honoré Laval in 1938 and described by Buck had apparently already become obsolete.

After "ransacking" the Society Islands in the 1920s for evidence of "native methods of plaiting," Willowdean Handy found that "only on small, isolated Maupiti households may still be said to carry on the native arts and crafts as part of the daily routine." There she

saw a number of coconut frond baskets but was aware of only one made of pandanus; a flat check-weave satchel with braided bottom closure that she said was then in decline. Also made on Tubuai, it was of the same genre more actively made in the nearby Cook Islands. Similar styles had been collected earlier. Roger Rose describes a pandanus satchel collected from Huahine shortly before 1822 that exhibited vertical twill plaiting, whipped top, and wide-braided bottom. It is now housed at the Canterbury Museum in Christchurch, New Zealand. Adrienne Kaeppler lists several flat satchels collected on the Cook voyages that were plaited in blocks of horizontal and vertical twill, with a top edge defined with loops for holding a drawstring. These would seem to represent just a small part of the variety of baskets once made, as indicated by the many basket names listed in Edmund and Irene Andrews' 1944 Tahitian/English dictionary.

Most of the basket-making activity in 1930s French Polynesia appeared to occur in the Tuamotu Archipelago, where a goodly variety of coconut frond and pandanus baskets was collected by Emory for the Bishop Museum. He brought back five kinds of small temporary coconut frond baskets called *mongini*. Three of these were the same as those described by Handy for the Society Islands. He also collected flat, 4-strip, keel-bottomed baskets called *mono hāparu* and a more capacious type, called *kero,* which is described below. The pandanus baskets he collected came in a number of shapes (flat or boxy), weaves (check or twill), and finishes (serrated, braided, or level tops), and with continuous or braided bottoms. Despite this great diversity, descriptions of names listed for baskets in Stimson and Marshall's *Dictionary of Some Tuamotu Dialects* would lead us to believe that the craft was even richer in the past.

The coconut frond baskets collected and described by Bishop Museum anthropologists are listed in the table on page 84.

We know little about precontact baskets. Statements in journals of Captain Cook and his crew are generally limited to such observations as noting that

A view of the Island of Ulietea, Tahiti, as pictured in
Hawkesworth's *Account*. This eighteenth-century
drawing of Tahiti shows baskets in canoes, set on shore
for receiving fish, and carried in hand. *Photo courtesy of
Bishop Museum.*

coconut and pandanus baskets were made in "a thousand different designs" for "multifarious" uses. Sidney Parkinson, artist on Cook's first voyage, also mentioned that a sort of basket was made from the "rind of the trunk" of the banana. Freycinetia baskets, especially, must have caught the fancy of those early observers, because they depicted them in drawings (figure, page 90) and recorded some details about them. We are told that the baskets were hung from the ceiling when used to store food and utensils and were carried on canoes for fishing. They called the basket *heenei*. This is probably *hina'i* in today's orthography. The manufacture of this tightly twined globular basket continued at least through the 1920s in Tubuai, and in Tahiti where Handy observed a similar version, then called *ha'apua*. They were made large for containing shrimp and small for carrying and hanging in the house. Another twined form of freycinetia basket was distinguished by having widely spaced rows and carrying handles. Handy observed a flat satchel of this type in 1920. Rose observed another similar but rectangular-bottomed one, now in the collection of the Peabody Museum, that was collected in the 1890s.

Most contemporary baskets are sold in the small craft shops scattered thoughout Pape'ete, Tahiti, the capital of French Polynesia. The baskets are made locally by women originally from other islands of French Polynesia. Judging by the subtle variation of basket shapes and patterns from store to store, each shop would seem to have its own artisans. The items offered for sale represent a revival of the craft of pandanus plaiting in French Polynesia and a standardization of the basket styles throughout the region.

Pandanus purses and shopping bags are the predominant articles. One especially is widely used by local shoppers. Called *'ete* (figure 56), it is woven with a half-width leaf, has right-angle checker weave, a narrow rectangular bottom, and decorative flat braid attached to the top edge. Other pandanus baskets seen today range from change purses to 50-cm-high boxes. All are plaited in check. Some have the surface enlivened by inserted strips of the dark brown wild banana bark and some by pandanus strips wrapped through the plaiting (figure 57). Finer articles are accented by the use of a twist and plait technique that makes the texture nearly lacy (figure 55).

Modern use of coconut frond baskets is not as obvious in Tahiti as in other parts of Polynesia. To demonstrate to visitors the continued viability of the craft, the government tourist office sometimes sponsors weaving demonstrations. Participants are women born on the islands of the Austral and Tuamotu groups. They weave small temporary coconut baskets—some for holding flowers or light objects and others for wrapping food to be cooked in earth ovens. The ladies turn out an amazing variety of these baskets in rapid succession.

The baskets they make are *'ō'ini*, which are unique to eastern Polynesia. *'Ō'ini* are made from two, four, or eight short strips of great rib with only two to four leaflets clinging to each. Pairs are interwoven, or intersected then interwoven before being plaited with each other. Slight variations in the ways leaflets are worked result in different shapes that make special uses possible. For example, the *'ō'ini menemene* (figure 54), with its decorative round shape, is often given to guests to take home food after weddings. It can also be covered with flowers inserted through the plaiting, then hung as a decoration. The use of a semiclosed *'ō'ini* for storage is a signal that the user does not want anyone else to use the contents. The open rectangular *'ō'ini* (figure 53) has been found convenient for use as a woman's purse. In Tubuai the *'ō'ini* continues to be employed for holding food while it cooks in underground ovens (umu). These cooking *'ō'ini* may be made by men or women.

Finishing details vary with the region. In the Marquesas Islands, for example, the round *'ō'ini* is finished by combining the leaflets that close the two sides into a 2-ply twist or 3-ply braid and then bringing those tails up to the handle on the outside. Elsewhere these same leaflets may be carried up to the handle on the inside or simply connected straight across the bottom.

Split- (figure 1) and unsplit-rib baskets like those seen in the 1920s in Tahiti are still made today. Both are called *ha'ape'e*. Also still extant is the 2-strip keel basket from Tubuai (figures 51, 52) called *'ete nī'au* (coconut leaf basket) that is used for collecting and washing coffee beans and carrying food from the bush. A similar basket is made today on Rangiroa in the Tuamotus. Since there is no earlier documentation in published literature for this basket on Rangiroa or for the braided U-shaped basket recently observed in the Marquesas island of Fatu Hiva, their antiquity in those regions is not clear.

A fine coconut basket, called *kero* (figure 50), continues to be made in the Tuamotu Archipelago. It has two quite unusual characteristics. Instead of commencing with the usual strips made of leaflets still connected by great rib material, this basket has strips made up of separate, thinly cut leaflets that have been connected by braiding their base ends together. Only in the flat, decorated kete ngahengahe (color plate 7) once made on the Cook island of Manihiki was this combining technique used outside of French Polynesia for baskets.

It is, however, commonly employed today for making coconut leaflet midrib brooms in Fiji, Tonga, and the southern Cook Islands. The other unusual characteristic of the Tuamotu basket has to do with the bottom. It is flat, usually defined by four corners, and has no braid of any kind. Its pattern is a continuation of the vertical twill of the sides. Identical baskets were made in the Austral Islands at least since the early twentieth century. Similar baskets with keel bottom closing have also been made.

Figure 49. **Contemporary pandanus basket. Tahiti.**
This basket, made only in French Polynesia, and popular in the eastern Tuamotu Archipelago for carrying tobacco, is plaited from full-width leaves. This style basket can be made as large as 33 cm high.
14 × 14 cm wide × 20 cm high

French Polynesian Coconut Frond Baskets

Island Group	Type	Name	Use
Society	4 kinds of 4-strip 'ō'ini	'ō'ini	cooking containers
	4 kinds of 8-strip 'ō'ini	'ō'ini	carrying raw food and flowers
	split-rib top, single braid closing	ha'ape'e pahai	carrying fruit
	unsplit rib bottom with French braid opening	ha'ape'e aua ha	carrying heavy loads
	2-strip basket, keel closing	'ara 'iri	carrying
	4-strip basket, keel closing	'ara 'ri; ancient name: 'arapapa	carrying
	single-strip basket, French roll keel closing	ha'ape'e	carrying heavy loads
	full-leaf, U-shape, French roll closed sides	ha'ape'e	
	full-leaf, U-shape, sides French braided and bound into a mesh	ufara	carrying heavy loads
Austral	4-strip or braided multi-leaf start, vertical twill, square bottom	Tuamotu weave	
	8-strip 'ō'ini	'ō'ini	
	split-rib basket, French braid or roll keel closing		carrying food from garden umu cooking
	2-strip basket, 1- or 2-braid keel closing	'ete nī'au	
	4-strip basket, keel closing		
Tuamotu	'ō'ini; 2 kinds of 2-strip, 1 kind of 4-strip, and 2 kinds of 8-strip	mōngini	
	4-strip basket, keel closing	mono hāparu	
	4-strip or braided multiple-leaflet start, vertical twill sides, flat 4- or 6-cornered bottoms	kero	
Marquesas	8-strip round 'ō'ini	kaoho	carrying fruit
	4-strip basket, keel closing	hakete	carrying fish

Sources: Handy 1927, Aitken 1930, Linton 1923, and Bishop Museum collection.

Figure 50. **Kero. Tuamotu Islands.**
Two views of one kind of traditional Tuamotuan kero.
Note the 4-corner, non-braid bottom. This basket is also
made in hexagonal and rectangular shapes. *Basket
courtesy of Toni Han.*
*15 cm diameter × 15 cm high, 20 cm diameter ×
20 cm high*

Figure 51. **Ha'ape'e. Tubuai.**
A traditional 2-strip coconut basket used for carrying coffee. Note the still-shiny surface of this newly woven basket.
46 cm long × 33 cm wide × 29 cm high

Figure 52.
Inside view of the basket shown in Figure 51 revealing
the first-course French braid typical of most keel-bottom
baskets.

Figure 53. ʻŌʻini. French Polynesia.
This traditional form has been used for umu cooking and
for carrying light loads. In the Tuamotus the leaflets are
split, midribs removed, and each half-leaflet plaited
separately.
23 cm long × 3 cm wide × 17 cm high

Figure 54. **'Ō'ini. French Polynesia.**
Made from eight 3-leaflet strips, this small traditional
basket is commonly used for carrying flowers and,
covered with flowers, for decoration. This type of basket
is also used in the Cook Islands for carrying small, light
objects and collecting shellfish.
30 cm long × 22 cm wide × 21 cm high

Some Tahitian objects as depicted in Parkinson's *Journal*. Of object no. 6 he writes, "One of their baskets; round the mouth is a kind of netting made of plaited twine, through which a string is put, which draws the plaiting together, and closes up the mouth. It is 11 inches high and 3 feet in circumference." Original drawing by S. H. Grimm. *Photo courtesy of Bishop Museum.*

Figure 55. **Pandanus baskets. French Polynesia.**
Shopping bag on left (38 cm wide × 33 cm high) is woven
from full-width, unstripped pandanus leaves. The purse
(28 cm long × 5.5 cm wide × 22 cm high) is closed with a
zipper and lined with a small, coarse, check-woven
basket that creates inside compartments.

Figure 56. **'Ete. French Polynesia.**
This pandanus basket is the shopping bag most
commonly seen in Papeete today. *Basket courtesy
of Yosihiko Sinoto.*
43 cm wide × 34 cm high

Figure 57. **Pandanus purses. French Polynesia.**
These modern purses are accented with wild banana
skin and smocking. The 3-ply pointed braid sewn to the
rim of the smaller basket is common in French Polynesia.
Similar examples have been collected for the last
hundred years. *Basket on left courtesy of Toni Han.*
26 cm long × 8 cm wide × 18 cm high, 22 cm long ×
7 cm wide × 14 cm high

Pandanus coil basket. Samoa.
22 and 17 cm wide × 15 cm high

··AFTERWORD··

Why do indigenous crafts interest people of technological societies? Prestige, nostalgia, guilt, boredom, as well as genuine appreciation, have been suggested as reasons by Nelson Graburn in his book on ethnic arts. Other factors might be idle curiosity, scholarly interest, and a desire to make contact of a sort with another culture.

In a way, viewing traditional crafts is like looking at an old family photograph. The person we see may not be known to us but we are still somehow connected. Likewise, no ethnic artifact is ever completely alien to us, for in any of the areas of materials, techniques, or functions a common ground may be found. The familiar embedded in the unfamiliar creates a kind of cultural bridge that leads to awareness of the adaptability, inventiveness, competency, and artistic ability inherent in all peoples.

Indigenous crafts interest not only those outside the culture, but also the descendents of the original artisans. For them the bridge is not between cultures, but between the past and the future. When accomplishments of past eras live on as part of daily life or have been preserved through collection and documentation, the possibility of perpetuating time-honored craft forms even after years of disuse is assured.

To protect this now-fragile heritage, additional work needs to be done in several areas. One is fieldwork on isolated islands. This could bring to light forms and methods we thought had disappeared. It would surely supplement our knowledge of distribution of styles. It might even finally lay to rest the tantalizing rumors of the plaiting prowess of present-day women on out-of-the-way islets. Any study of living basket makers should include capturing the working process itself on video to preserve the nuances as well as the techniques themselves.

Needed to complement fieldwork is a survey of holdings of those museums whose Pacific island baskets, collected during the last two hundred years, have not yet been described in published sources. Old dictionaries and early writings hint at a wealth of basket types not widely known today. Perhaps by scouring those museums that acquired objects from early voyagers or their heirs, from other collections, and from more recent scientific expeditions, some of those missing links might be discovered and a more complete picture emerge.

Linguists might bring another dimension to the picture. Across the expanse of Polynesia and sometimes beyond, cognates of the chief basketry terms are used. Tracking the subtle changes in sound, meaning, and multiple meanings, as well as geographic distributions of these terms, would surely enable us to gain additional insight into the relationships among these regions.

In precontact times ethnic arts were firmly integrated into the web of culture and were a necessary part of everyday life. Today traditional practices are increasingly seen as a hindrance to economic advancement and are being abandoned by the younger generations. It is my hope that this book will contribute to an increased awareness and appreciation of Polynesian baskets and that it will assist in the perpetuation of this once fundamental aspect of island life and cultural identity.

Pandanus storage basket. Fiji.
A contemporary pandanus basket made with a coarse
check lining and inside stiffeners of bamboo. The technique of whipping edges is said to date from the 1950s.
38 cm long × 22 cm wide × 46 cm high

··TECHNIQUES··

The methods used for handling tropical materials have been relatively unknown outside their immediate sphere of use. This is because most craft books are written by and for persons residing in temperate regions. Even existing ethnographic materials describe but a few of the ways objects included in this book are made. This dearth of information not only hampers complete understanding of individual baskets, but also seriously inhibits comparative study. In addition, the absence of associated terminology in English makes communicating about construction a ponderous exercise.

Most of the coconut leaf plaiting and commencing techniques presented in this chapter have never appeared in print before and have no English names or native names that easily lend themselves to translation. I have therefore given them monikers which, if inelegant, do focus directly on the pertinent characteristics of the methods involved.

No attempt is made here to show how baskets are shaped or assembled beyond what has been indicated in preceding chapters. That is subject enough for another work. Additional details for specific regions may be gained from some of the ethnographies listed in the bibliography.

"Feejee Baskets, etc.," from Wilkes' *Narrative. Photo courtesy of Bishop Museum.*

··COCONUT FROND WORK··

The coconut frond is the most commonly used material for making work baskets in central Polynesia. Techniques used throughout the region are the commencing techniques of single leaflet twist and same-strip leaflet twist, the lifting method of plaiting, and French braid. The remainder of the techniques appear to be specific to Fiji.

COMMENCING TECHNIQUES

Fine coconut leaf baskets are generally made of two or four strips taken from both sides of the coconut frond. The usual commencing technique twists together the leaflets of the strips from one side of the frond before plaiting these with the leaflets of the opposite strip(s). This technique strengthens the edge while making it decorative.

Double Leaflet Twist
A pair of leaflets (one from each strip) twists over the next pair.

Single Leaflet Twist
Each leaflet of a single strip twists over the next.

Alternating Strip Leaflet Twist
Each leaflet of a pair of strips twists over the next of the other strip.

Same-Strip Leaflet Twist
Each leaflet of a pair of strips twists over the next of its own strip while passing those of the other strip.

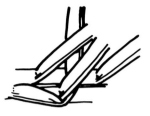  

Parallel-Strip Leaflet Twist
Each leaflet of a pair of strips twists over the next of its own strip without passing those of the other strip.

LIFTING TECHNIQUES

In the most common method of coconut frond plaiting, horizontal bands of diagonal weaving are continuously added until the desired depth is reached. The most popular method of working is the lifting technique in which one group of leaflets always remains dominant; it is on top when a row of plaiting begins and is still on top at the finish of that row. This technique is very much like that used for plaiting pandanus.

Here is how it works. A group of the dominant leaflets is lifted out of the way, the appropriate number of opposing leaflets for the pattern lifted, one or two leaflets of the dominant group dropped down, and the leaflets from the subordinate group dropped across them. Then the plaiting proceeds opposite the direction of the dominant group. Within a pattern the ways the leaflets are handled do not vary from one row to the next.

Usually the leaflets of the dominant group are sinistrals and the subordinate group, dextrals. (In order to address the specific characteristics of Polynesian basketry and mat making, Buck [1930] coined these words. Dextrals are those elements that incline to the right and usually function as warps. Sinistrals are those having tips extending to the left and generally serve as wefts.) This technique easily lends itself to horizontal, vertical, and leaning vertical twills.

Horizontal Twill

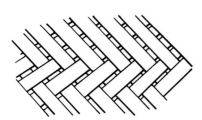

A band of horizontal twill ready for a new row.

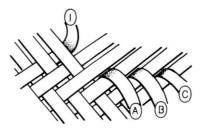

A group of sinistrals and a dextral are lifted.

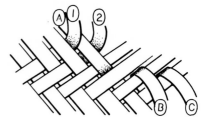

The left sinistral (A) is dropped, then a new dextral (2) to the right of the original is lifted.

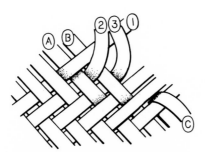

The next sinistral (B) is dropped, followed by the left dextral (1). Then the next dextral on the right (3) is lifted.

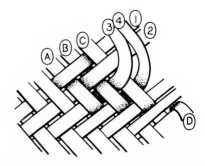

The previous step is repeated through the end of the row.

Vertical Twill

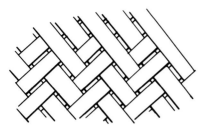

A band of vertical twill ready for a new row.

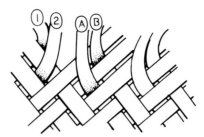

A group of sinistrals and two dextrals are lifted.

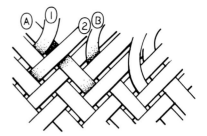

The left sinistral (A) is dropped, followed by the dextral on the right (2).

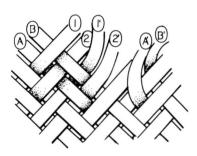

The next sinistral (B) is dropped, followed by the remaining dextral (1). Two new dextrals are lifted.

The left sinistral (A'), then the right dextral (2') are dropped. The next dextral to the left (2) is lifted.

The next sinistral (B'), then both remaining dextrals (1' and 2) are dropped. Two new dextrals are lifted to repeat the sequence from the previous step.

Vertical Twill—Lift One, Put Two Version

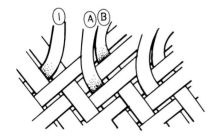

A group of sinistrals and one dextral are lifted. Two of the sinistrals (A and B) are dropped.

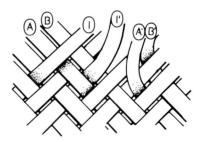

The dextral (1) is dropped and the pattern continues by lifting the second dextral to the right.

Leaning Vertical Twill

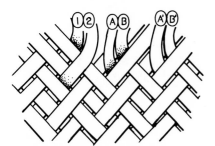 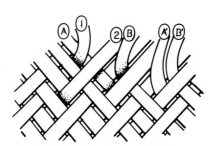 

A group of sinistrals and two dextrals are lifted.

The left sinistral (A) is dropped, followed by the dextral on the right (2).

The next sinistral (B) is dropped, followed by the remaining dextral (1). Two new dextrals are lifted. Repeat from previous step.

FRENCH BRAID
A French braid is a 3-ply braid with new elements added (usually) after each turn.

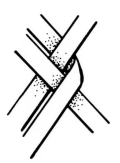   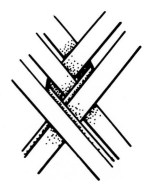

Kete. Viti Levu, Fiji.
A 4-strip coconut frond basket with leaning vertical
twill and horizontal twill.
42.5 cm long × 27 cm wide × 29.5 cm high

LIFT AND SWITCH TECHNIQUE

In this variation of the lifting technique, the direction of the dominant group switches from one row to the next. Here only the necessary number of leaflets of the dominant group are lifted. Then the needed number of opposing leaflets are pulled out from under, the two groups are interleaved in the proper order for the pattern, and dropped. The plaiting continues in the direction of the dominant. The interleaving pattern usually changes with alternate rows. This technique easily lends itself to horizontal, vertical, and leaning vertical twills.

2/2 Vertical Twill

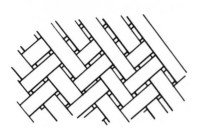

A band of vertical twill with sinistrals dominant.

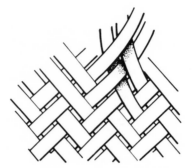

Two dominants are lifted. Two opposing leaflets are pulled out. The left sinistral is slipped under both dextrals and the right one crosses over the closest dextral and under the next. Leaflets are dropped and process continues to the left.

Repeat.

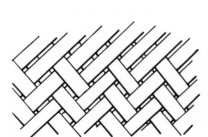

The pattern ready for the return. Dextrals now dominant.

Two dominants and two opposing leaflets are raised. The sinistral on the left is placed over the other two leaflets and the right one is slipped under the first and over the second. Leaflets are dropped and process continues to the right.

Repeat.

Leaning Vertical Twill

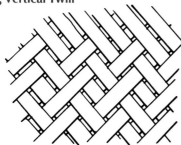

A band of leaning vertical twill with sinistrals dominant.

Two dominants are lifted. Two opposing leaflets are pulled out. The left sinistral is slipped under both dextrals and the right one is crossed over the closest dextral and under the next. Leaflets are dropped and process is continued to the left.

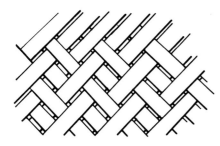

Alternate row; dextrals dominant.

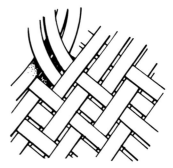

Two dominants are lifted up and two opposing leaflets pulled out. Both sinistrals are crossed over both dextrals. Leaflets are dropped and process continued to the right.

2/2 Horizontal Twill

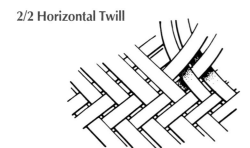

Two dominant leaflets (sinistrals) are lifted. Two opposing leaflets are pulled out. The sinistral on the left is slipped over the first dextral and under the next. The remaining sinistral is placed under both dextrals. Leaflets are dropped and process is continued in the direction of the dominant.

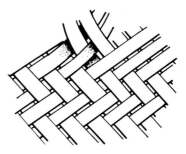

Alternate row; dextrals dominant. Two dominant leaflets are lifted. Two opposing leaflets are pulled out. The sinistral on the left is slipped under and over the other two leaflets. The second sinistral is slipped over both dextrals. Process continues in the direction of the dominant.

PUSH DOWN TECHNIQUE

In this technique each leaflet in turn of the dominant group is simply pushed down through the subordinate group where desired. Dominant and direction of plaiting switch with each row. This is a handy technique for setting up a horizontal twill, doubling up leaflets, or reversing the direction of the dominant group.

Horizontal Twill

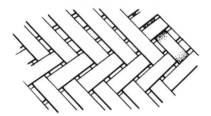 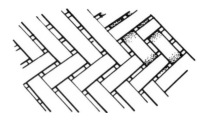 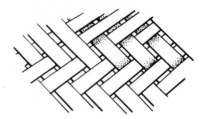

PULL AND PUSH TECHNIQUE

Each leaflet of the subordinate group is first pulled up through the recumbent dominant group, then pushed down through it again the appropriate number of crossings forward. From this same interstice the next leaflet (usually the second one over) is drawn. This technique nicely lends itself to vertical, leaning vertical, and skip twills. Where the first leaflet is pulled up determines the type of twill. This process has also been used in Kapingamarangi for doubling up leaflets.

Skip Twill

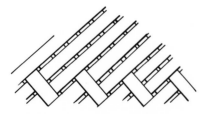 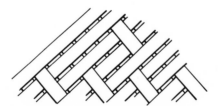 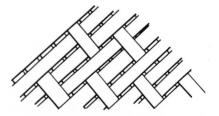

A band of plaiting ready for the next row.

The desired dextral is pulled up from between the appropriate sinistrals and pressed down two or three leaflet crossings forward.

Moving to the right, the next appropriate dextral is pulled out and the process repeated.

Kete. Ovalau, Fiji.
This coconut frond basket has an oval flat bottom closed
with two French braids. It is plaited in skip twill and
vertical twill.
37.5 cm long × 32 cm wide × 20 cm high

Throughout the Pacific basin pandanus leaves are used in the making of mats and baskets. The most common pattern is the check or plain weave. The strips are arranged at right angles to each other and usually at diagonals to the edge. Plaiting is usually built up in bands roughly 12 cm wide. The terminology in the following description is adapted from that introduced by Peter Buck in his *Samoan Material Culture*. This same technique is used when plaiting coconut fronds in the check pattern.

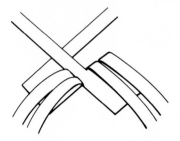
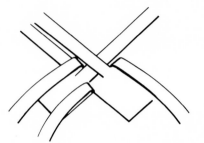
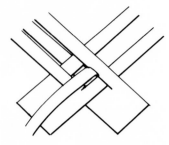

(1) Half-leaves are usually stripped 0.3 to 2 cm wide to about 10 cm of the end. This unstripped portion holds the commencing edge in a stable manner until the plaiting is finished. Then it will be stripped and combined in a complex sort of French braid. Strips are folded back to get them out of the way. The left strip of the dextral leaf is extended forward. The left strip of the sinistral crosses it.

(2) The first strip is folded back. This secures the just-worked sinistral. The next dextral to the right is laid down and the next sinistral to the right laid across it.

(3) Now the first dextral is once again extended forward, the just-worked one folded back, and the last one laid down. Finally, the third sinistral is extended across.

Adding half-leaves as needed, this procedure continues until the working edge is about 15 cm long. From then on, whenever the top dextral reaches the recumbent position, it is left down and no longer plaited.

As each new sinistral is placed in the space created by the raised and lowered dextrals (the shed) it is held firmly and under tension with the left hand as the right hand alternately raises and lowers those dextrals while moving from left to right.

In order not to have the left edge loosen during the plaiting process, it is temporarily locked. The usual manner is to turn each dominant sinistral up and to the right just after it has been worked. This accumulation of turned strips holds the edge effectively in a temporary manner without interfering with the plaiting.

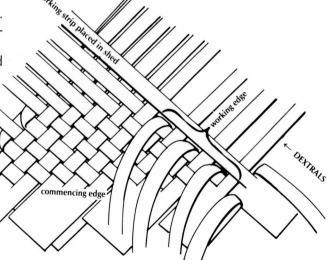

Contemporary pandanus purse. Fiji.
The black-and-white pattern on this check-weave basket
results from the color sequence of the strips.
24 cm long × 5.5 cm wide × 21.5 cm high

··COIL TECHNIQUE KNOTS··

SINGLE-FACE

Tonga

inside

outside

Samoa

inside

outside

DOUBLE-FACE

Tonga

inside

outside

Niue

outside

Pandanus coil basket. Vava'u, Tonga.
Solidly worked on a core of coconut leaflet midribs, the
controlled shape of this basket reflects the skill of the
maker. The absence of pattern is unusual.
33 cm diameter × 32 cm high

Starting the bottom

Two strips are laid down. One at a time, two more are placed across, then locked into place by their crossing. Additional crosses are added until the length of the base is established. Additional horizontals may be added to make the base wider. Each new horizontal is locked by lifting and dropping it or the crossing strips to continue the one-under, one-over pattern.

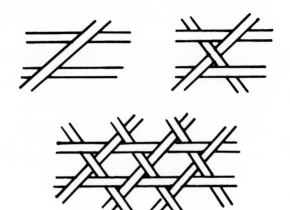

Starting the sides

A new horizontal goes all the way around and overlaps itself. This causes all the strips it crosses to fold up. The sides are built up by continuing with the same technique used for adding bottom horizontals.

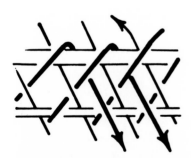

Defining the top edge and working back on the sides
Moving to the right, the dextrals slip around the top multiple horizontal and rest on the front of the mesh.

Top continued
A sinistral rounds the top to slip under its opposite number.

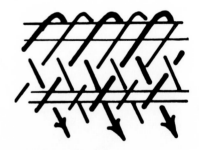

Side continued
Dextrals are inserted in back of the horizontal before returning to the front to continue interlacing.

Noke. Viti Levu, Fiji.
Traditional women's fishing baskets. Both are worked in the 3-strand lattice-work technique with reinforced walls. Note that the locking method for the reinforcing horizontal is slightly different for the two baskets.
Left: made of vere in Savu on the eastern coast of Viti Levu. *37 cm wide × 21 cm high*
Right: made of wame in the upland interior village of Lutu. *21 cm long × 38 cm high*

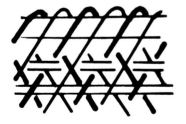

When the sides are to be reinforced, a new horizontal is introduced between the old horizontals and is held in place by the newly crossing diagonals.

113

A view of the island of Ulietea, Tahiti, as pictured in
Hawkesworth's *Account. Photo courtesy of Bishop
Museum.*

··BIBLIOGRAPHY··

Aitken, Robert T. *Ethnology of Tubuai.* Bishop Museum Bulletin 70. Honolulu, 1930.

Andrews, Edmund, and Irene Andrews. *A Comparative Dictionary of the Tahitian Language.* Chicago: Chicago Academy of Sciences, 1944.

Arbeit, Wendy. *What Are Fronds For?* Honolulu: University of Hawaii Press, 1985.

Beaglehole, Ernest, and Pearl Beaglehole. *Ethnology of Pukapuka.* Bishop Museum Bulletin 150. Honolulu, 1938.

Brigham, William T. "Mat and Basket Weaving of the Ancient Hawaiians." *Bernice Pauahi Bishop Museum Memoirs,* vol. 2, no. 1. Honolulu, 1906.

Buck, Peter H. (Te Rangi Hiroa). *Arts and Crafts of the Cook Islands.* Bishop Museum Bulletin 179. Honolulu, 1944.

———. *Arts and Crafts of Hawaii.* Bishop Museum Special Publication 45. Honolulu, 1957.

———. *Ethnology of Mangareva.* Bishop Museum Bulletin 157. Honolulu, 1938.

———. *Ethnology of Manihiki and Rakahanga.* Bishop Museum Bulletin 99. Honolulu, 1932.

———. *Ethnology of Tongareva.* Bishop Museum Bulletin 92. Honolulu, 1932.

———. *Material Culture of Cook Islands (Aitutaki).* Memoirs of the Board of Maori Ethnological Research, vol. 1. New Plymouth, N.Z., 1927.

———. *Material Culture of Kapingamarangi.* Bishop Museum Bulletin 200. Honolulu, 1950.

———. *Old Polynesian Curios.* Bishop Museum Bulletin 197. Honolulu, 1948.

———. *Samoan Material Culture.* Bishop Museum Bulletin 75. Honolulu, 1930.

Burrows, Edwin G. *Ethnology of Futuna.* Bishop Museum Bulletin 138. Honolulu, 1936.

———. *Ethnology of Uvea (Wallis Island).* Bishop Museum Bulletin 145. Honolulu, 1937.

Cook, James. *A Voyage Towards the South Pole and Round the World . . . 1772–1775.* London, 1777.

Edge-Partington, James. *An Album of the Weapons, Tools, Ornaments, Articles of Dress etc., of the Natives of the Pacific Islands.* Manchester, England, 1890–1898.

Graburn, Nelson H. H. (editor). *Ethnic and Tourist Arts.* Berkeley: University of California Press, 1977.

Handy, Willowdean Chatterson. *Handicrafts of the Society Islands.* Bishop Museum Bulletin 42. Honolulu, 1927.

Hawkesworth, John. *An Account of the Voyages Undertaken . . . for Making Discoveries in the Southern Hemisphere. . . .* London: W. Strahan, 1773.

Kaeppler, Adrienne L. "Anthropology and the United States Exploring Expedition." In *Magnificent Voyagers: The U. S. Exploring Expedition, 1838–1842,* edited by Herman J. Viola and Carolyn Margolis. Washington, D.C.: Smithsonian Institution Press, 1985.

———. "Artificial Curiosities." Bishop Museum Special Publication 65. Honolulu, 1978.

———. (editor). *Cook Voyage Artifacts in Leningrad, Berne and Florence Museums.* Bishop Museum Special Publication 66. Honolulu, 1978.

Koch, Gerd. *The Material Culture of Kiribati.* [Translation of *Materielle Kultur der Gilbert-Inseln,* 1965.] Suva, Fiji: Institute of Pacific Studies, University of the South Pacific, 1986.

———. *The Material Culture of Tuvalu.* [Translation of *Die Materielle Kultur der Ellice-Inseln,* 1961.] Suva, Fiji: Institute of Pacific Studies, University of the South Pacific, 1983.

———. *Südsee-Gestern und Heute. . . .* Brunswick, Germany: A. Limbach, 1955.

Linton, Ralph. "Material Culture of the Marquesas Islands." *Bernice Pauahi Bishop Museum Memoirs,* vol. 8, no. 5. Honolulu, 1923.

Loeb, Edwin M. *History and Tradition of Niue.* Bishop Museum Bulletin 32. Honolulu, 1926.

Macgregor, Gordon. *Ethnology of Tokelau Islands.* Bishop Museum Bulletin 146. Honolulu, 1937.

McKern, W. C. "Tongan Material Culture." Unpublished manuscript at Bishop Museum, Honolulu (192–).

Mafi, Tupou Veiongo. *Tala 'o e Lalanga Faka-Tonga.* Nuku'alofa, Tonga, 1986. (In Tongan.)

Motteler, Lee S. *Pacific Island Names.* Bishop Museum Miscellaneous Publication 34. Honolulu, 1986.

Parham, John W. *Plants of Fiji Islands.* Suva, Fiji: Government Press, 1964.

Parkinson, Sidney. *Journal of a Voyage to the South Seas in His Majesty's Ship the Endeavour.* London, 1773.

Pendergrast, Mick. *Feathers & Fibre.* Auckland, N.Z.: Penguin Books, 1984.

———. *Te Mahi Kete—Maori Basketry for Beginners.* Auckland, N.Z.: Reed Methuan, 1986.

Rose, Roger G. "Material Culture of Ancient Tahiti." Ph.D. dissertation, Harvard University, 1971.

Speiser, Felix. *Ethnographische Materialien aus den Neuen Hebriden und den Banks-Inseln.* Berlin: C. W. Kreidel, 1923.

Stimson, J. Frank, and Donald Stanley Marshall. *Dictionary of Some Tuomotu Dialects of the Polynesian Languages.* Peabody Museum of Salem, Massachusetts, 1964.

Wilkes, Charles. *Narrative of the United States Exploring Expedition,* vol. 5. Philadelphia: C. Sherman, 1844.

About the Author

Wendy Arbeit received a B.A. degree from Temple University and an M.A. in fine arts from Columbia University. She has taught courses on crafting in various media but specializes in the weaving of natural materials. Her accomplishments also include illustration and book design, of which this volume is an example. Ms. Arbeit studied the indigenous crafts of the American Indian before turning her attention to Oceania. Her previous book, *What Are Fronds For?*, introduces the craft of Pacific Basin coconut plaiting to beginners. For the present book, she spent six months traveling throughout the South Pacific researching the design, construction, and use of baskets.

About the Photographer

Douglas Peebles graduated from Florida State University with a B.A. degree in mass communications. He has since been communicating his love and understanding of his adopted home, Hawaii, through his photography. His photographs illustrate eight previous books, including *Kauai, A Many Splendored Island* and *Pua Nani: Hawaii Is a Garden*, and numerous magazine articles. He maintains an extensive stock photo file on Hawaii.